TOURISM MATTERS

Study Guide for
BTEC Travel and Tourism

DAVID SPURLING

authorHOUSE®

AuthorHouse™ UK
1663 Liberty Drive
Bloomington, IN 47403 USA
www.authorhouse.co.uk
Phone: 0800.197.4150

Published by AuthorHouse 01/18/2018

ISBN: 978-1-5462-8436-9 (sc)
ISBN: 978-1-5462-8437-6 (e)

Print information available on the last page.

This book is printed on acid-free paper.

Tourism Matters: Study Guide for BTEC Travel and Tourism

David Spurling B.Sc., P.G.C.E, D.G.A, F.C.I.L.T., M.Inst.T.A

John Spurling BSc (Hons), DipTP, PGDip (Law), PGDip (CMI), MRTPI, MCMI

Acknowledgements:

I would like to thank Poppy Cole for providing the idea for this book; without her, this book would never have been written. Many people made substantial contributions to early draft and have provided invaluable advice throughout the project. I would like to thank Marcus Dean and Jackie Davidson for their insights into the tourism industry and for their help during the editing process. And I would like to say a special thank you to my wife, Anthea, who has always encouraged me with her unwavering support and patience.

Table of Contents

1. Introduction to the Tourism Industry

1.10 Definition of tourism industry

The Concise Oxford Dictionary describes tourism as organised touring. It defines a tour as a journey through a country from place to place. The World Tourism Organisation defines tourism as an activity where people travel to, and stay in, new or uncommon places for them. People may travel for pleasure, business, family visiting, or other reasons. Tourism includes both long stays and short stays, even a day trip. Tourism can be domestic, with people from the same country visiting other parts of the country; or it may be international, with visitors from other countries. Therefore, the types of tourism are:

The Roman Baths at Bath are a popular tourist destination

- Domestic tourism: A domestic tourist is someone who visits his or her own country. For example, if you live in London you might spend a day in Bath visiting the Roman sites, or go for a longer trip in the Lake District; in both cases you are a domestic tourist. Officially, visitors who travel only for a day are called 'day visitors', and the term 'tourist' properly applies for visitors who stay at least one night in their destination. These terms are usually found in statistics.

1.20 different types of tourism and definition

- Outbound tourism: This term applies to anyone who travels to another country different from his or her own. For example, if you live in the UK and visit Germany.
- Inbound tourism: people who travel to the UK from other countries perform inbound tourism. Inbound tourism is always from the perspective of the hosting country.

There are different types of travel according to the purpose of the travel. We mostly talk about leisure and business travel:

- Leisure travel: traveling for pleasure is still the most common reason for travelling. This kind of travel includes day trips, short breaks, holidays and long stays, family visits, shopping and special events.

Often people have to travel for business

- Business travel: there are four main types of business travel. These are meetings, incentive travel, conferences, and events. Meetings are very important for business as businesspeople might work in different locations and countries but eventually they often need to hold face-to-face meetings. For this reason, they need to travel to another country, and hold meetings in, for example, hotel meeting rooms. Incentive travel is a reward and acknowledgement of good business performance. Conferences are larger meetings where people from different businesses meet to discuss issues. They usually last more than one day, and often take place at hotels. Events are usually one day, or less, and they are more specific. A business event may consist in launching a new product, or try to get external funding.

Another term used in tourism is 'specialist travel', which consists in specific activities during travel such as:

- Adventure tourism (outdoor activities)
- Health (spa)
- Education (going to Italy for an Art History course)
- Cultural heritage (historical sites)
- Dark tourism (visiting concentration camps or visiting jails)
- Voluntary work (doing voluntary work in African schools)
- Conservation (restoring old churches in Lithuania)
- Eco-tourism (environment-friendly tourism such as rural tourism)

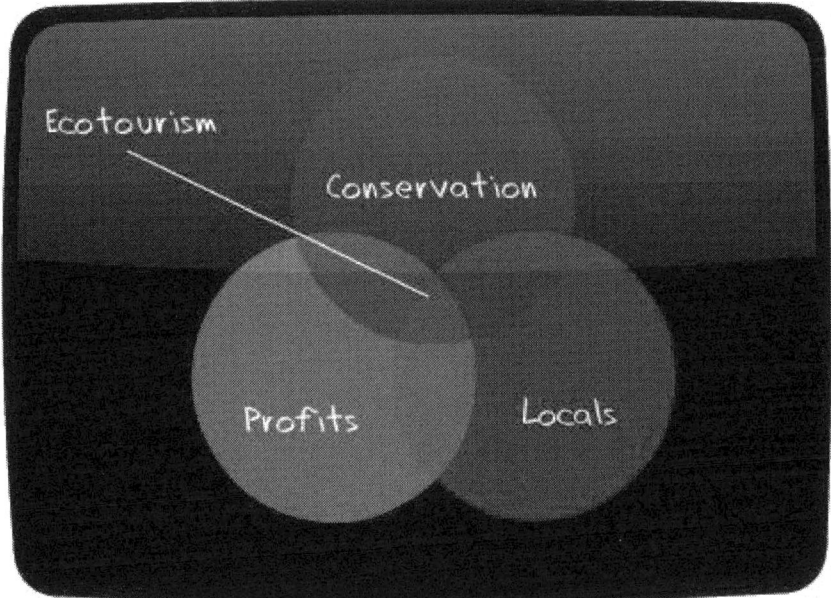

Sustainable tourism is concerned with the impact of tourism on the environment. Tourism can negatively affect the environment in several ways. For example, hotels on the seaside might be built too close to the coast and damage the landscape as well as contribute to the contamination of the sea through big scale human activities. Therefore, sustainable tourism aims at minimising negative environmental impacts on touristic sites, creating economic benefits for the locals, conserving and respecting local culture, and promoting the integration of tourists in the hosting community.

Sustainable tourism is very positive and has the following benefits for the planet:

- Environmental protection: Some organisations, such as English Heritage, are deeply committed to protecting historic buildings, and an important part of their mission is to preserve historical sites.
- Links with the local community: locals also benefit from local regeneration, and they can also obtain special fees to visit their local sites of interest. New attractions might be created both for tourists and locals.
- Reduced energy consumption: energy can be saved in different ways. Some hotels ask their clients to use towels more than once in order to save energy on washing. Lights can be switched off if rooms are not in use. Solar panels can be installed as well as heat extractors.
- Reducing waste: recycling is very common and can be widely used in many ways. For example, hotels and organisations can re-use carton or plastic products.
- Cost savings: tourism organisations can reduce costs by recycling or saving energy.

- Competitive edge and image: being a green business creates a good reputation for business as nowadays sustainability is highly regarded. Some customers may only travel with green organisations.

1.40 The importance of the tourism sector to the UK economy

Overseas residents' visits to the UK by month
March 2014 to March 2017

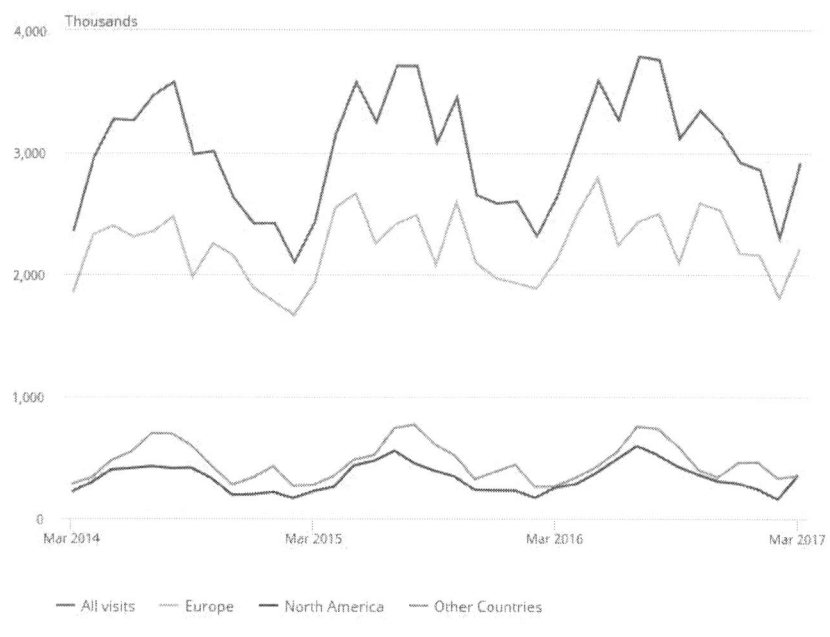

Source: International Passenger Survey (IPS) – Office for National Statistics

The table tells us how many visitors have come to the UK between March 2014 and March 2017. The table also gives us a clear idea of the countries of origin of the inbound travellers. In this way, we know that American visitors are the most common, and the tourist market can focus either on increasing their number, or try to attract visitors from other countries.

This information is very important in order to know how much tourism impacts on the Gross Domestic Product (GDP). Travel and tourism helps GDP as it brings in revenue to the economy. In 2015 overseas inbound tourists spent £22.1 billion.

Regarding domestic tourism, in 2015 domestic tourism meant an expenditure of £19.6 billion. You can find more information about British domestic tourism here: https://www.visitbritain.org/gb-tourism-survey-2015-overview.

1.50 Employment

The tourist sector creates a significant number of jobs. In 2014, 2.97 million people were employed in the tourism sector. Some of the jobs are direct, which means that they are directly related to the sector, and it includes any kind of travel and tourism organisation. Other jobs are indirect, and these include industries that support the sector as construction of hotels. All the indirect jobs are part of the so called 'economic multiplier effect'. This name designates all the income provided by direct activities that is destined to related activities. For example, if a tourist goes to Cornwall and buys an item in a shop, the shop benefits from tourism. The owner or employee of the shop can in turn spend this money on something else. All this generates economy.

1.60 Industries in the Tourism Sector

There are different kinds of industries in the tourism sector:

- Tour operators: these are companies that organise package holidays. They liaise with all the parts involved in a holiday: transport, accommodation, guided tours, etc. Tour operators offer the whole holidays organised from beginning to end. The holidays can be sold through travel agents or directly to the customers online or by telephone. There are three kinds of tour operators:

  1. Domestic: these companies provide packaged holidays within the UK for UK customers.
  2. Outbound: these companies organise holidays abroad.
  3. Inbound: these companies are found in the country of destination and organise holidays for the visitors. For example, inbound companies in the UK package holidays for foreigners coming to visit the country.

1.70 Travel agents:

- Travel agents book holidays organised by tour operators, and then sell them to their customers. However, nowadays travel agents experience a lot of competition from online agents, tour operators selling direct, and customers booking their holidays by themselves. In order to remain competitive travel agents need to offer excellent customer service as well as increase their services. It is then not rare for travel agents to offer services such as arranging insurance and providing foreign exchange services. Travel agents do not only deal with packages but they can also help customers to book individual services such as booking flights, hotels, or tours.

1.80 Online travel services

- Online travel services: Almost all tourism companies use a website to sell their products, as the Internet is highly used by customers to book their holidays. There are online versions of travel books and guides, as well as information and reviews on destinations. There are online consolidators such as booking.com, or lastminute.com. These are companies that sell services from other companies (hotels, transport).

1.90 Passenger transport

Passenger transport: Road transport is very popular for domestic tourism as most people travel by road or train. Coach holiday companies also offer organised trips. The UK national rail network is owned by Network Rail but the trains are run by private train-operating companies. There are 24 different train-operating companies in the UK, for example East Coast. Air services are provided by different airlines; flights can be domestic or international. Health and safety in air travel is strictly regulated by the Civil Aviation Authority. Scheduled airlines

Many people travel by coach to reach tourist destinations

are airlines which offer full service; this means that ticket prices include food, drinks and a baggage allowance. In long haul flights entertainment is also available. British Airways is an example of scheduled airline. Low-cost scheduled airlines, such as Easy Jet, offer cheaper ticket prices but these do not include services such as free food or drinks. The customer needs to pay extra if he/she wishes to consume. Chartered airlines are less common as they operate flights for holiday schedules. Sea travel is also important; cruising, for example, is particularly popular among retired people.

1.100 Accommodation

- The most common types of accommodation are hotels, guest-houses and bed and breakfast, apartments, youth hostels, and camping. Hotels can be owned independently or be part of a wider chain. Some hotels also have facilities for business customers, others have spa facilities. Guest houses and bed and breakfasts are more local and typical from the place. They are not usually part of a chain. Apartments are the most similar option to be in one's own place, as they have the customary rooms: kitchen, bathroom, living room, and bedrooms. It is very practicable for families with children. They can cook themselves too. Youth hostels are very cheap. They are run by the Youth Hostel Association (YHA). Finally, camping offer diverse options such as a space for the tent or fully equipped static caravans.

1.110 Visitor attractions

- Visitor attractions include many kinds of entertainment from fun visits to natural or cultural tours. The most common categories for visitor attractions are natural attractions, which include beaches, mountains, lakes and rivers, forests, and caves; purpose-built attractions, which include theme parks, museums and galleries, resorts like Disneyland Paris, rides like the London Eye, and venues like the O2 arena. Finally, heritage, which includes historical attractions such as Stonehenge. Many natural attractions are protected, and visitors need to behave in a respectful way for the environment. Purpose-built attractions are purposely built to attract visitors.

1.120 Arts and entertainment
- These are events such as exhibits, concerts, or sport events. There are one-off events such as the London 2012 Olympics and Paralympics, and there are annual events such as Wimbledon and the tennis tournament, Chinese New Year, or the Edinburgh Tattoo. There are also festivals that attract visitors such as the Edinburgh Festival.

1.130 Key organisations in the travel and tourism sector
There are some organisations that provide support to the tourism industry: they represent their interests, or offer services that add to the value of the holiday package.

- Trade and professional bodies: They represent the interests of the bodies' members either to the government in order to influence policy, or to the media to achieve a positive public opinion. Trade and professional bodies also provide guidelines on how to operate to the tourism industry. Some of these bodies are the Civil Aviation Authority (CAA), the Office of Rail Regulation (ORR), the Association of British Travel Agents (ABTA), the Association of Independent Tour Operators (AITO), and UK Inbound. The CAA makes sure that UK airlines, airports and National Air Traffic Services (NATS) comply with all the safety regulations. The ORR makes sure that the rail industry complies with its regulations. The ABTA represents travel agents and offers guidelines for their operations. The AITO represents independent and specialized tour operators. UK Inbound represents tour operators that organise tours in the UK for inbound visitors.

- Ancillary organisations: These organisations provide additional services for tourists, for example, car hire, travel insurance, airport services, or event booking.

1.140 Product comparison providers
Some websites, such as Go Compare, allow the customer to compare rates and prices from different companies for the same product.

1.150 Types of organisation in the travel and tourism sector
Organisations in the tourism sector are funded in different ways. This depends on the aims of the organisation, as one might be more interested in profit than the other. Organisations can be private, public and voluntary. Most tourism organisations are private. They might be owned by an individual, by partners or by shareholders. The main aim of a private organisation is to make profit, which in this case, is done by selling holidays products. Public organisations are funded and run by the government. Even if public organisations make a profit, their main aim is to promote tourism. Voluntary organisations are usually charities. They are primarily involved in government policy and education.

1.160 The relationships between travel and tourism organisations
- Common ownership: There are two kinds of common ownership. The first one is 'vertical integration', which takes place when a business at one level of the chain of distribution merges with another business at another level of the chain. For example, if a tour operator owns an airline there is a common ownership. Secondly, 'horizontal integration' takes place when a business merges with a business at the same level of the chain of distribution. For example, if different tour operators are bought by one big tour operator, there is a horizontal integration.

- Commercial partnerships: There are partnerships between different organisations, which benefit each other. For example, a theme park can offer a discount to a visitor if he/she hires a car from a specific car hire organisation. Or a hotel might have offers on a nearby restaurant.

1.170 Consumer technology

Technology is widely used by the tourist sector, and has an impact on travel:

- Airports: Technology is used in both self-service check-in and security. Self-service check-in machines allow passengers to print out their flight ticket themselves without need to go to the check-in desk. There is also the possibility to check-in online from home and go to the airport with the flight ticket. For security purposes technology is absolutely necessary, as there are X-ray machines, chip and trace, etc.

- Visitor attractions: Technology is used to enhance the visitor's experience. For example, in a science museum the visitor can actively participate in the display through interactive technology. Audio guides, for example, are also popular in churches and cathedrals, or museums.

1.180 Accommodation
- It can be booked online using, of course, technology. In high standard hotels the rooms' lights and TV, for example, can be controlled through a touchscreen. At reception, hotels use technology to check in guests.

1.190 Websites:
- Almost any kind of travel and tourism organisation or service has a website where the visitor can find all the necessary information.

Chapter 2. Accommodation

There are a wide variety of types of accommodation for tourists to choose from. They can choose from hotels, guesthouses, farm centres, holiday camps, youth hostels, camping and self-catering accommodation. Accommodation can be classified in several ways: independent or part of a chain, commercial or non-commercial, static or mobile, urban or rural. The most common and wide classification is as serviced or non-serviced.

2.10 Serviced accommodation

In these cases, services, such as meals, breakfast, and cleaning, are provided with at least an overnight stay. The category of serviced accommodation includes hotels, B&B, motels, guesthouses, inns, youth hostels and farm guesthouses.

Hotels can be part of a chain or individually run. Hotel chains, such as NH or Marriott Hotels, benefit from economies of scale when it comes to purchasing, marketing, and recruitment.

2.20 Non-serviced accommodation

This classification includes all rented premises used for holiday purposes without services included, such as self-catering centres and villages, caravan, camping, self-catering young hostels, second homes, and boats. This type of accommodation is more flexible and economic.

2.30 Cruises

Liner cruises are particularly used by older people. The range of prices between the most luxurious and these in the cheapest parts of the ship can be enormous. There will also be tremendous seasonal variations. It is also sometimes possible to be one of the few passengers travelling on a cargo vessel which is allowed to carry up to 12 passengers with fewer regulations.

Liner cruises are very popular on more sheltered waters.

Some tourists will prefer to use simple boats with minimal accommodation. Many others will cruise on the inland waterways where they are usually quite safe.

2.40 House swapping holidays

Some people also choose to swap accommodation with each other, for example, through the Guardian house swap or Christian house and church swap. The Intevac house swap organisation claims to be the oldest of its type since it was founded in 1953. It will give details of the houses or accommodation provided including details of occupations as well as other relevant data.

2.50 Center Parks and contrast with other holidays

Center Parks offer warm accommodation and surroundings, which will satisfy some people, whilst at the other extreme are extreme holidays such as these which Ben Fogel illustrates on some of his Channel 5 programmes.

2.60 The demand for accommodation

The demand for accommodation is a derived demand. It depends upon demand for tourism as a whole i.e. it depends whether or not people wish to go away on holiday, and on the length of time that they wish to spend doing this. Most countries before the credit crunch 2007 had rising incomes for the majority of the population. Similarly, the amount of leisure time is often increased with the reduction in the number of hours worked.

2.70 Age of tourists

The demand for one type of accommodation rather than another may also depend upon the age of the holidaymaker. Older people may require accommodation which is easily accessible rather than having to walk up several flights of stairs especially if they are disabled. Older people may generally be less inclined to "rough it" rather than younger people. Older people may therefore prefer a comfortable bed in a guesthouse or hotel.

2.80 Income

People receiving high wages, or on a high pension, are much more likely to be willing to stay in a hotel or guesthouse than a student paying higher tuition fees who cannot afford such luxury. Data about incomes in the UK can be found from the census 2011.

2.90 Seasonal fluctuations

Because there are seasonal fluctuations in the demand for tourism, there are consequently seasonal fluctuations in demand for accommodation. The demand, therefore, for accommodation at cheap sites and camps may fall off almost completely in the winter. Conference traffic especially for smaller organisations, which cannot afford large sums of money, is therefore very helpful since the marginal costs of providing such accommodation are usually very small especially in the off-peak season.

However, demand for major cities, such as London, Paris, Vienna, or Rome, may remain more constant as the cities are also important centres for business executives.

2.100 Weekly fluctuations

Business executives usually require accommodation during the week and not at weekends which is one of the reasons why students looking at different prices will notice that quite often Eurostar, for example, will offer rates which are much cheaper at weekends than during the week to places such as Brussels and Paris.

2.110 The supply of accommodation

The supply of beds in a hotel is limited by the number of rooms, although where people are willing to share rooms, supply can be increased. Given the amount of space available, youth hostels, which have dormitory accommodation, can accommodate more people than hotels.

The supply of beds in a hotel is limited by the number of rooms

In crowded areas, such as central London, the cost of building materials as well as planning restrictions limit the extent to which hotels and guesthouses can expand the supply of accommodation. This is particularly true of countries such as Singapore, where the supply of land is limited. It is much less true of countries such as Australia where urban sprawl means that land is often available on the outskirts of the major cities.

Before the credit crunch 2007 onwards, many hotels and other accommodation were being built across much of Europe. After that period, far fewer hotels were built in many countries, and some hotels and guesthouses were abandoned during the process of construction. This particularly applied to some countries, such as the Republic of Ireland, Spain, Portugal and Greece. Within the European Union there have been problems for several countries and in 2017 this also applied to Italy.

Costs of some buildings have been affected by health and safety legislation which people often complain about in the short run. However, in the longer run it is extremely important as many disasters have shown.

Planning permission is very important in many countries. Farmers have often wished to supplement their income in a variety of different ways and particularly where ground is relatively infertile they will be pleased to be able to let campers have some form of accommodation. Similarly, many farmers are quite prepared to host campers if they are allowed to have caravans on their sites. In the UK, there are often restrictions on the number of months where people are allowed to stay in caravan accommodation. Typically, people are not allowed to live in them full-time.

The cost of labour also affects the supply of accommodation. If there is a vast supply of cheap labour willing to work in hotels or guesthouses, then hotel owners will be much more willing to take more guests. Following the British referendum on the withdrawal from the European Union in 2016, there are concerns that there will be fewer people willing to work in the lower paid jobs in hotels, such as cleaning, which are often done by overseas staff. Given the low pay, which exists in many of these jobs, if the economy is booming in one area, then the hotels and guesthouses will find it difficult to obtain suitable staff. On the other hand, in a recession or in an area, which has few other opportunities for workers, they will find it much easier to recruit suitable staff. Cornwall is an area which has high rates of unemployment generally partly due to its relative remoteness. Therefore, it is usually easy for the tourist industry to be able to find suitable staff.

2.120 Universities extending their use of premises

Universities and other forms of higher education often use their premises during the summer holidays and, therefore, they often wish to hire out their rooms and other accommodation to suitably responsible people. Smaller organisations in particular will often find it convenient to have conferences where there are lecture theatres and suitable equipment including microphones in order to enjoy a conference knowing that they do not have the administrative problems often associated with organising them.

Some universities, such as Oxford and Cambridge, are tourist attractions in their own right, and, therefore, they will find it quite easy to attract people to come to their campuses.

2.130 Visits by families to students and vice versa
As the number of students has risen considerably in England and Wales in spite of tuition fees and the absence of grants many families want to see their children whilst at university, and this may help the tourist trade. Some colleges have had accommodation on site to try to encourage people to come to the campus.

2.140 Why do tourists demand one type of accommodation rather than another?
Different types of accommodation vary according to price, degree of luxury, accessibility and services offered.

2.150 Price
The most important reason for wishing to go camping or youth hostelling rather than staying in luxury hotels for many people is the price. The price charged for pitching a tent or a caravan in a recognised campsite can be only a few pounds per person per night. The same is true of many youth hostels which, in spite of the name, cater for a wide variety of ages.

The price range can vary considerably according to the season. For this reason, offers vary: they can advertise a particular area in February at a very cheap rate whereas the same area in August might charge four times the price.

2.160 Degree of luxury
The price difference between different types of accommodation is often largely explained by the degree of luxury provided. The more amenities provided, the higher are the costs faced by the owners. Many campsites and youth hostels provide only basic washing facilities. These people requiring ensuite facilities would not usually wish to stay in a guesthouse. It is much cheaper to provide communal basic washing facilities than to provide several ensuite bathrooms which take up valuable room that could otherwise be used to provide more sleeping facilities.

Guests would expect to pay more for private bathrooms. Hotels and B&B also tend to provide a greater deal of personal service than other forms of accommodation. Guests are often willing to pay more for the ambience of the accommodation and this can account for some of the differences in price even when the services are similar.

The size of the room provided can vary considerably and therefore some people prefer camping in a tent or even caravans where there can be much more space than a typical youth hostel. Modern caravans often have a great deal of facilities including widescreen televisions as well as Wi-Fi suit in case some people wish to keep in touch with what is happening elsewhere.

Some youth hostels only provide dormitory accommodation which will not suit people who desire more privacy.

2.170 Convenience

The type of accommodation available may depend upon the location. Generally staying in an expensive area such as the West End in London will be very expensive whereas staying in the North East of England in the rundown former mining areas will be much cheaper.

Areas such as Hartlepool are aware of the rundown image. They have therefore used the Re-creation of an 18th century seaport which features the HMS Trincomalee, fightingships, a historic quayside, the Museum of Hartlepool and the P.S.S. Wingfield Castle, a former Humber estuary ferry.

2.180 Touring holidays

Some people like to go on touring holidays where they can travel overnight on trains or coaches, and then leave the daytime free to enjoy sightseeing.

2.190 Camping

Hikers often find camping convenient whilst other people will not enjoy carrying a tent around with them. Some campsites are however very luxurious and the term Glamping meaning glamorous camping has recently come into general usage.

Youth hostels are not always convenient but websites enable people to establish when they need to arrive at the hostel in order to reserve a bed for the night. Some youth hostels have insisted on people arriving at a particular time in order to book their accommodation overnight; other have required lights to be out by a certain time which is not necessarily convenient for the people who enjoy nightlife once on holiday. Similarly, however, many hostels and some guesthouses also set the latest time before locking up their accommodation.

Chapter 3. Tour Operations and Travel Agents

3.10 Who are the tour operators?

Thomas Cook was one of the earliest travel agencies in the UK, originally founded in 1841.

Tour operators are wholesalers that sell their holiday packages. This can be done online or via travel agents. Travel agents are the retailers from who they purchase transport for their clients, such as coach trips, river or sea trips. They can also arrange packages much more cheaply than if their customers buy them for themselves. Many customers may prefer to use package holidays rather than having the inconvenience of arranging their own packages especially if they are unfamiliar with the language of the country of destination.

Tour operators are in a position to buy holidays in bulk which makes purchasing cheaper than if guests try to arrange their own packages.

There are many famous tour operators. Thomas Cook was the person who, in 1841, hired a train to carry a temperance party from Leicester to Loughborough a distance of around 10 miles. After this Thomas Cook has been a famous name in most high streets in the United Kingdom.

Some famous tour operators have, however, run into difficulties partly because of changing tastes and partly sometimes because of overstretching their resources. Lowcostholidays, for example, went bankrupt in 2016.

3.20 Types of tour operators
There are four main categories to classify tour operators:

- Mass-market operators: They sell a lot of holiday packages. Examples of these are Thomson Holidays and Thomas Cook.
- Specialist operators: These operators offer a more individualised experience to customers. They also work on more specific and detailed destinations or kind of holidays; for example, a specialist operator might only offer adventure holidays.
- Domestic operators: These package for domestic markets, for example, for Britons staying within the UK. These are often short holidays.
- Incoming tour operators: These operators plan holidays within a country for foreign visitors. For example, for Japanese tourists visiting the UK.

3.30 Costs of providing services

Some hotel chains, such as Premier Inn, operate in many towns and cities throughout the UK, and often charge per room rather than according to the number of occupants. Therefore, for many families, who are willing to share their room with their children, this is an attractive proposition. Some hotel chains only provide accommodation, in effect subcontracting out meals to the local restaurant.

If children are accommodated in the same room, more people can be accommodated within a single space.

3.40 Chartering an aeroplane

Many tour operators charter a plane which means that they have exclusive use of a plane for a particular flight. The advantage of this, from the tour operator's viewpoint, is that they can sometimes fly directly to destinations which other tour operators cannot do. The other advantage is that with bulk purchase it is cheaper per passenger than if seats had to be booked separately. Sometimes the charterer can book the size of the aircraft which they prefer rather than the standard size aircraft. Sometimes they may be able to arrange the seating to suit their clients' needs, rather than having a standard configuration.

However, the cost of chartering an aeroplane will be the same per passenger since most children require their own seats. Similarly, the administrative costs will be virtually the same, regardless of the number of passengers. The savings are usually even greater if the child is under two so that they can sit on their parents' lap during the flight.

Usually tour operators will charge slightly less for children in hotels rather than for adults. The table below shows a hypothetical tour operators costs per week:

	Booked adults	Child	Standby passenger
Chartering aeroplane	£500	£500	Zero
Hotel	£420	£420	£420
Travel agents commission	£120	£90	?
Office costs	£66	£66	£10
Total	£1106	£1076	

| Profit | £72 | £72 | £75 |

3.50 Pricing policy

It is assumed that tour operators are aiming for profit maximisation.

The example in table 1 demonstrates that profit for each individual passenger is £72 and similarly for each child. If, therefore, the tour operator has 50 passengers on each flight, then the total profit would be £3600.

If the tour operator wanted to increase the profits overall to £4500, it would require £18 more from each individual passenger. However, the tour operator will need to take account of the price elasticity of demand. Price elasticity of demand can be calculated by

$$\frac{Percentage\ change\ in\ demand}{Percentage\ change\ in\ price} \times 100$$

<u>Percentage change in demand x 100%</u>
Percentage change in price

Tour operators will generally increase price if the demand is inelastic. They will reduce price if the demand is elastic but will need to take into account the elasticity of supply. Profit can be calculated by looking at total revenue minus total costs. The level of maximum profit is determined by the interaction of supply and demand. For example, on the supply side a decline in the exchange rate of the pound, which occurred after the European referendum vote in 2016, may force the tour operators to add a surcharge. A surcharge is an additional charge to that published in the tour operator's brochure or website.

Some countries have experienced very high rates of inflation which means that the prices of their hotels, guesthouses and food will have risen considerably which will be reflected in the costs tour operators have to contend with.

3.60 Seasonal demand

If the tour operator chartered a hundred-seat aircraft every day of the year, and the same sized hotel every day of the year, the cost of supplying holidays to adult per passenger would be the same all round. If in January the tour operator only gets 20 booked adult passengers, then they will almost certainly not be able to make a profit. Therefore, during the off-peak season tour operators will probably charge a much lower price than in the high season. Students looking at any brochure from tourist operators will observe considerable differences.

Sometimes tour operators will try to offset seasonal trends especially for these with longer holidays by offering flights to countries such as Australia and New Zealand. The high costs of flights will be reduced per head the longer the holiday.

From the UK operator's viewpoint, many British people have a poor command of other languages. For this reason, Australia and New Zealand make it easier to market these countries than others where people may feel more uncomfortable with their poor linguistic skills.

3.70 Demographic factors
The United Kingdom now has more people over the age of 60 than under the age of 16, so tour operators who wish to have a long-term business plan will take account of this.

Saga holidays has had a niche market for people over the age of 50. They won awards in 2013 and 2015 for best special interest holiday companies.

3.80 Multiple destinations
Whilst many tour operators have only offered a single destination some holidaymakers may prefer to go to several different destinations. For example, American visitors may wish to visit London, Paris and Vienna during their stay. They can now use websites, and often arrange this for themselves. The digital revolution has made it easier for individual travellers to check on prices of a range of accommodation as well as booking up individual coach trips such as travelling on a double-decker bus in London.

The London Big Bus Company for example offers a hop on, hop off service covering the main London attractions. This will include Trafalgar Square, Mayfair, and Big Ben which is next to the Houses of Parliament. The bus operators also often offer commentaries in several different languages which is helpful to many visitors.

3.90 Walking tours
Many tour operators will also include a walking tour as part of the package. Erna Low, which claims to be the oldest tour operator in the United Kingdom, included this event in the 1960s as part of their personalised approach from the tour guide during their stay. The advantage of a tour guide, who knows the party well, is that he or she does not have to repeat the same itinerary every time if he or she knows that some itineraries will not please customers.

3.100 Advantages and disadvantages of the tour operators
Tour operators buying in bulk often make it much cheaper for a consumer than if they were to try to arrange it themselves. However, there will be an element of profit charged by the tour operator which may reduce this advantage.

Going on a holiday arranged by a tour operator avoids the need to search for information about travel and accommodation, and also usually guarantees that the accommodation will be available.

Many tour operators belong to ABTA, the Association of British Travel Agents, which offers security in the event of financial problems.

3.110 Insurance
Most operators will insist that customers have insurance especially if they are travelling abroad.

Some people will have their own insurance which covers sickness whilst on holiday abroad. Many passengers will also require insurance on luggage especially if travelling abroad. Details about insurance costs can usually be found on tour operator's websites.

3.120 Advantages to hotels

If hotels are selected by tour operators as a base for their holidays, the hotel has a greater degree of certainty about demand. Block bookings have many advantages as they reduce the administrative costs. If the tour operator uses the hotel considerably, the hotel, in effect, may become a subsidiary of the tour operator even though it is still nominally independent. However, block bookings may mean that the hotel is unable to take advantage of individual holidaymakers who might be prepared to spend more money.

Some tour operators may specialise in major events such as weddings, since the amount of money spent on a typical wedding can be very considerable.

3.130 Advantages to travel agents

Holiday packages arranged by tour operator travel agents have lower administrative costs than if they had to arrange travel themselves.

3.140 Air Travel Organisers' Licensing (ATOL)

Tour operators wishing to operate scheduled or chartered air tours abroad will obtain an Air Travel Organiser's Licence from the Civil Aviation Authority.

3.150 Inclusive tours

Inclusive tours are the name given to packaged holidays. This means that the tour operator arranges both travel and accommodation, as well as optional trips to entertainment such as theatre, opera or sporting events.

Many operators provided tours to Brazil during the Olympics and Paralympics in 2016. Similarly, large numbers of people visited the UK during the Olympics and Paralympics in 2012.

3.160 Rail packages

When British rail was a nationalised industry it offered golden rail packages to many hotels at holiday resorts. Since denationalisation in 1994, the private operators have continued this tradition, and with the opening of the Channel

The Orient Express is a luxurious way to travel by train.

Tunnel, offer a wider choice of destinations than before. Eurostar itself offers a wide range of destinations using its own services and many other operators offer similar packages. For January 2017, Eurostar offered a single fare to any station in Belgium via Brussels for a minimum fare of £31 per head including taxes for standard class. Passengers requiring first-class luxury accommodation would pay considerably more.

Some offer escorted tours which can be helpful for people who are uncomfortable with other languages. It may also be helpful for simple things such as knowing where luggage can be stored for a short time or knowing the location of the nearest toilets. An increase in terrorist incidents around the world has led to additional waiting times at airports. Time spent at railway stations is usually less.

3.170 Air packages

Many people like air packages which provide a wide variety of holiday destinations and with longer duration, at very reasonable costs.

Scheduled services may be used by tour operators to arrange tour excursions. These packages may be sold individually to tourists. On any scheduled flight, there may be only a few seats available to the tour operator, whereas when a tour operator chartered aircraft, especially the tour operator has to try to fill all the seats. Inclusive excursion packages are more flexible than inclusive tours by charter.

They are often high-quality products giving high quality accommodation to customers. In contrast, the more common inclusive tours using charter flights cater for the mass market.

3.180 Travel agents

These can be part of a chain or individually owned. Lately, the number of multiple agencies (agencies owned by a single company) has increased. The two main multiple agencies in the UK are Thomas Cook and Thomson. Each of these companies is owned by a tour operator (vertical integration).

3.190 Retail travel agents

These specialise in selling holidays including flights and ancillary services (insurance, car hire, theatre tickets, etc.). Travel agencies have reduced in number as more people choose to book their holidays online.

3.200 Business travel agents

They specialise in travel bookings for business people. These might need to travel in very short notice, and they often require premium services in flights and hotels.

3.210 Online travel agents

Many travel agencies have an online site as customers now use to book their holidays online. Although travel agencies maintain their traditional face-to-face services in high street premises, many customers now use online travel agencies.

Chapter 4. Customer service

It is important for tour operators to provide excellent customer service.

Customer service is all that an organisation does to meet or exceed customers' expectations, and, thus, produces customer satisfaction. There are some key statements to remember when it comes to customer satisfaction:

- Meeting the customer's needs
- Exceeding the customers' needs
- Being attentive and helpful
- Being concerned and honest
- Making the customer happy to return
- The customer enjoys the experience

All the above points guarantee that a customer will return, and that you will build up a fixed number of customers. Through network marketing, customers tell others about their good experience, and you may gain more customers in this way. It is also very rewarding to know that one is providing excellent customer service; that makes employees feel happy and satisfied with their jobs.

4.10 What are the components of customer service?
Customer service has three components:

- Product or service: This is what the customer buys (a flight ticket, a theatre ticket, booking a hotel room).
- Processes and procedures: These are all the steps necessary to purchase/book the product (for example, the website steps from the beginning to the checking out).

- Personal behaviour: This refers to the behaviour from the people who are offering you the products or services.

An organisation increases its benefits by providing an excellent customer service, as they gain more customers.

4.20 Customer types

There are two main types of customers:

- Internal customers: These are the customers you work with in order to enhance your service for external customers. Internal customers include colleagues with whom you work, managers, directors, owners, staff at other places, and suppliers. All internal customers constitute a chain in the customer service delivery chain; therefore, it is very important that each of the parts involved do their job very well.
- External customers: These are the ones who buy or book the organisation's services. There are eleven big groups in which external customers can be classified:
    1. New customers: An organisation must always attract new customers, not only when the business starts. The first step towards gaining and keeping new customers is being able to understand them.
    2. Existing customers: If customers are happy, pleased and satisfied with the organisation's services, they are most likely to remain with you and continue using your services. The organisation, however, still needs to put the same effort in knowing existing customers as they may change tastes and preferences over time.
    3. Individuals: Individual customers may wish to be on their own for the entire duration of their holiday, or they may prefer to socialise and meet others. In the last case, if you are a hotel, for example, make sure you try to introduce him or her to other customers.
    4. Groups: Some customers travel in groups. Some groups are organised groups, for example, retired people groups. Organised groups have a leader, who is the one who communicates with the agency or organisation. The leader might usually also communicate individual travellers' needs.
    5. Families: This is one of the most common types of customers. They are particularly important during school holidays.
    6. Couples: Couples may travel alone or with other couples. In the first case, they might like to join activities with others, while in the second case, each of the couples might like to enjoy some private moments. You need to take care of these preferences, and meet the customers' expectations.
    7. Special interests: Some customers might be particularly interested in specific activities, such as dancing or water skiing. You need to find the best option to meet their needs and budget.
    8. Business travellers: These customers usually want quick and efficient customer service at short notice. Be aware that international business people might deal with jetlag. This might change their needs. It is good for them to have quiet rooms in the hotels.
    9. Age groups: Customers' ages need to be considered in order to provide good services. For example, children might enjoy play areas, while old people might need some help

with physical issues. Also remember that the way in which you need to address different age groups changes: for children you might behave more informally, while adults might prefer a more formal style.

10. Culture and ethnicity: Customers' cultures and ethnicities might influence their needs, as well as their religious views. This might affect, for example, their choice of food such as Kosher or Halal food. In this case, you need to make sure that required menus are available.

11. These with additional physical needs: Disabilities need to be considered, and customers' needs to be met. Sometimes, this might only mean being patient and repeating the information to a customer with hearing difficulties; other times, a customer might need a wheelchair. The organisation needs to be ready to help and provide without delay.

4.30 Needs of different types of customers

You need to provide customers with:

- Accurate price information
- Health, safety, and security information
- Assistance
- Advice
- Products and services

As a tourism organisation, you need to be aware of your customer's needs, and find the best price-value option. For example, if you are an agent in a travel agency, you might receive a customer for whom it is very important to be in Brussels the day after by mid-afternoon. Therefore, you will need to focus on that instead of, say, the difference in price between going by train or airplane from London.

- Accurate information: Customers need detailed information in advance in order to be sure they want to purchase the product. Once during the holiday, they might wish to know other kinds of information, for example, on an activity's price they have just seen in the spot, or on directions to somewhere.

- Health, safety, and security: Customers need to know if they need to vaccinate before travelling, for example, to a tropical country. Some countries have insects that are very dangerous. Information on these kinds of issues can be found in the Foreign & Commonwealth Office (FCO) website. Other more minor issues, such as strong sea currents, must also be reported. Hotels, for example, have evacuation procedures in case there is a fire or any other cause for evacuation. Security is highly present, especially since the terrorist threat. Closed circuit television, for example, is very common.

- Assistance: Different people need different kinds of assistance and help. The elderly might need help with mobility, and parents might need childcare with their young children.
- Advice: Customers often ask for the advice of the hotel receptionist, or the travel agent to find out more about their destination, about restaurants, or alternative transport.
- Products and services: Be aware of your unique selling point. You need to present your products and services as unique and different from what others offer.

4.40 Responding to customer needs

There are two main kinds of requests: written and verbal. These are forms of communication between customer and organisation.

- Written requests: Email is the most commonly used form of communication. Many services have a request section in their websites for customers to leave their opinions, or ask for help. Letters are also a form of written request, and they present a more formal style than emails.
- Verbal requests: These are mostly face-to-face although they can also be by telephone. Staff must pay attention to what the customer is saying in order to be ready to help.
- Recognising unstated needs: You can also try to realise when the customer needs something before he or she lets you know, or even before the customer knows his or her own need. For example, some customers might not know they need a visa to go on holiday, but as a travel consultant you should know.

4.50 Customer service

- First impressions: First impressions are very important. The first moment of contact between customer and organisation is crucial to give the customer a positive feeling. The customer might purchase your services based on his or her first impressions.
- Personal presentation: First impressions take often place when the customer comes into your workplace. It is important to look clean, organised, and polite. The brand image is at stake here.
- Environment: Always try to imagine how the customer will perceive your workplace. Is it nice, clean, in order? To succeed in creating a good environment for your customers think of the following questions:
    1. How would you react if you went into a travel agency, and all the computers were switched off?
    2. How would you feel if you found the train's floor full of litter?
    3. What would you think if you entered a hotel lobby and there was no one at reception?

4.60 Skills and techniques:

1. Patience. You need patience to help and show your customer around. For example, if you are a resort manager, you need to explain everything to your new customers, and make sure they become familiar with the place (knowing where things are, meals schedules, etc.). That might need you to repeat things more than once as some people need time to become used to new environments.
2. Empathy. This skill allows you to put yourself in the place of your customer, and you can understand him or her better in his or her needs or problems.
3. Active listening. You need to make sure you listen carefully and understand what your customer is saying. Only then you can answer appropriately. You can show you are

listening by using verbal and non-verbal techniques; for example, you might nod, and make sure you remember the information the customer is giving you. In some situations, there might be background noise, and you still need to make sure you are listening to your customer. When customers talk to you all at once, you might need to ask to speak in turns.

4. Sensitivity. Customers have different sensitivity levels: some are very shy, others get angry quickly, others get easily upset. When dealing with these situations, you need to be aware of using the correct tone of voice, and show the adequate concern for your customers' requests. Confidentiality is another very important aspect of sensitivity. In fact, some issues you might need to deal with require confidentiality and absolute discretion, and only you and your customer will know about it.

5. Language. Language involves not only what we say but also how we say it, and how we use our body and gestures. It is important to use the right words, and make sure we do not use long sentences or complicated expressions. We should not use slang or jargon either unless we are sure that the customers understand the phrases. By modifying the tone and volume of our voice we can show interest and enthusiasm. Smiling is also a very important characteristic that makes us approachable and pleasant.

6. Teamwork. It is very important that everyone in the customer service chain does his or her job in an excellent way. Only then can the customer feel satisfied. In customer service, teamwork is usual, for instance a cabin crew must work as a team on an airplane.

- Policies: These enable an organisation to meet its aims. Each organisation has its own policies and standards. Mission statements describe the organisation's goals and values. Mission statements influence the policies and procedures as well as the recruitment and training policies. Policies create the framework for deciding what and how to sell. These policies include the regulation of the relationship between customers and staff. Policies can include information such as:

  1. What information can the organisation provide, as well as how and when will such information be provided.
  2. What level of performance it will aim at (punctuality, quality, response times).
  3. What to do if a service fails to be provided.
  4. The compensation they will provide in the above case.

- Impacts: You need to be clear with your customers about how your products benefit them. To do that you need to see which of your products better matches your customer's desires. This is in some way to find a solution for the customer.

- Technology: technology is a support to customer service. Technology helps both tourism professionals and customers by saving time and budget. By having customers booking their holidays online organisations save on commission charges to travel agencies. From the customer's point of view, for example, he or she saves time queuing at the check-in desk in the airport, as now it is possible to go to the check-in machines and print your flight ticket.

4.70 Principles of customer service

The most important principles for all tourism staff are:

- First impressions: The first time you get in touch with your customers makes a big impact on them. Your attitude influences their enjoyment of the holidays, or any service that you provide. Some organisations use a 'mystery shopper', an anonymous shopper that visits the organisation as customer, but he or she is really employed by the organisation in order to check how customers are being assisted.
- Company image: The brand image is very important for the success of the organisation. The company's image is built up in many different ways, for example, through the products the company sells, the good impression staff make on customers, or the website. Other things, such as the cleanliness of the offices in the case of a travel agency, for example, are also very important. Important behaviour rules, in order to build up a positive image, are not to criticise the organisation or your colleagues in front of customers, not to share confidential information, and not to lose your temper at work or drink alcohol and in the United Kingdom there are many restrictions now on smoking in the workplace.
- Speed and accuracy of service: Staff need to learn skills to provide a quick service and avoid customers waiting for long. Staff need excellent organisational skills, good keyboard skills, negotiation skills, research skills, and they should know their product very well.
- Consistency: Customers value consistency, that is, they want to see that everyone in the organisation conveys the same message, and that there is a sense of teamwork. In this case, if a customer cannot be assisted by a usual staff member, they can address someone else who will be able to follow up with the customer. Usually information is digitalized and is easy to access.
- Products and services offered: Staff should have good knowledge of the products that they are offering and selling. They should know the features and prices in detail. To achieve this, staff can participate in product training. Knowledgeable staff look very professional and build up a very positive image.
- Offering information and advice: Staff really make a difference if they can give advice on minor issues, such as when it is best to travel to the desired destination, which airports are better to fly to, which public transport to use, etc.
- Dealing with complaints: When things go wrong, for example, a delayed flight, staff should know how to deal with upset customers. For example, the company might offer a refund, or a check to spend in the airport's shops.

Communication skills

Communication skills are very important, and you need to know which method (verbal or written) is the most appropriate for each situation. Written communication is more formal than verbal communication, and written communication is used to confirm official decisions.

- Face-to-face communication: In many occasions staff deal face-to-face with customers, for example, in a travel agency, in a hotel, resort, etc. The main rules when speaking directly with a customer are:

1. Smile when you greet the customer.

2. Listen to the customer.

3. Make eye contact but do not stare.

4. You need to look interested.

5. Let the customer talk without interrupting him.

6. Keep the appropriate physical distance from the customer.

7. Thank the customer.

• Telephone: Communication by telephone is useful for quick inquiries, as neither of the parties involved need to wait for an email reply, for example. Things to be aware of when dealing with customers on the phone are:

1. Answer call quickly.

2. Answer the call with your name or/and the organization's name.

3. Have a nice tone.

4. Listen carefully to the caller.

5. Speak clearly.

6. Call back if you promise it.

• Written communication: Many times the easiest for a customer is to send an email to the organisation. Since the development of the internet, and since when almost everyone has access to a personal email, email writing is a very common type of communication. There are, however, other kinds of written communication such as that use for marketing purposes (leaflets, posters, cards), or press communication (press releases and articles). Complaints are also written down. If you use written communication you need to make sure that:

1. There are no spelling or grammar mistakes.

2. The message should be effectively conveyed.

3. The message should state to whom and by whom it is addressed, when it was received, and if any action has been taken.

4. The language used should be adequate for the addressed.

• Non-verbal communication: Body language complements what we say, and it can also give more information about ourselves. Non-verbal communication include:

1. Bodily contact; for example, shaking somebody's hand.

2. Physical proximity.

3. Orientation: Where people sit, for example, in a meeting in relation to their position in the company.

4. Posture.

5.   Gestures.

6.   Facial expressions.

4.90 Business skills

Staff need business skills as they need
to carry on administrative tasks.
Documentation is very important in the
tourism sector, and records need to be
updated for internal purposes. Staff
might need to report to external bodies
such as the HM Revenue and Customs
or the Health and Healthy Executive. IT
skills are also important as so many
things are done through computers, as
with the computerised reservation
systems (CRS).

4.100 Selling skills

Selling your product is key to the

Business skills are essential in the tourism sector.

success and future of your organisation. Selling is a structured activity, and you need to follow some
steps in order to be successful:

- Building rapport: Sellers need to be aware of the different needs of their customers, who have
  all different budgets and interests. Sellers need to be sympathetic and respectful of their
  customers' needs. Selling can be undertaken in many different places (shops, hotels,
  restaurants, at home, or in an office). In all these different locations, the same selling
  principles apply. Establishing rapport with the customer is very important in any case as it is a
  way to gain insight into the customer's needs.
- Establishing customer needs and expectations: You should help your customer to clearly state
  his or her wishes for the holidays. By establishing the customer's needs you can manage his
  or her expectations by clearly stating what option you have for him or her and what to expect
  of them. Expectations refer to what the customer expects from the product: he might think
  the hotel is very clean, and if it is not, they will be disappointed. For a travel agent, some
  questions are key to figuring out the customers' expectations:
  1. What is the size of the group travelling?
  2. How old are the children (if any) travelling?
  3. When and for how long do you want to travel?
  4. How do you want to travel?
  5. What is your budget?
  6. Do any of the travellers have special requirements?
- Features and benefits: After having clarified the customer's expectations, you present him or
  her with a product that you think matches the requirements. At this stage, you need to focus
  on the benefits and uniqueness of the product you are offering. You need to use three
  statements during the presentation of the product:

1. Features statement: You emphasise the characteristics of a product; for example, the facilities in a resort.
2. Advantages statement: You indicate the good side of the product in contrast to others. For example, a high-speed train arrives earlier or is much quicker than others even if they are more expensive.
3. Benefits statement: This specifically expresses how the product responds to the customer's needs, and why is this the best purchase option.

- Overcoming objections: After explaining the benefits of a product to your customer, he or she might still have doubts that you need to sort out. The customer might have doubts on the price, or the hotel, for example. You need to be able to offer other options, which again relates to your ability to identify the customer's expectations and needs.
- Closing the sale: Towards the end of the selling process you need to convince the customer to buy the product by trying to make the customer say things like 'I'd like to buy…' You also need to identify expressions of interest in the customer, such as 'this looks quite good' in order to build from there, and enhance your possibilities of selling.
- Completing documentation: After the sale, you need to ensure that all the documentation relating to the booking is appropriately done. This might include filling in a form, paying, issuing a receipt, and giving the customers the tickets he or she needs.
- After sale-service: This is important in order to have a returning customer. You need to be able to help the customer with further preparations such as emailing him or her a reminder of the flight's scheduled departure. Also, do not forget that a customer might have complaints after the holiday, and you need to be ready to help.

Chapter 5. UK as a Destination

The UK has three main types of tourism destinations: capital cities (London, Cardiff, Edinburgh, and Belfast), seaside resorts, and countryside areas. The capital cities are these of each of the four countries constituting the UK. They are the financial and cultural centres of the country. Some popular seaside resorts in the UK are Brighton, Weston-Super-Mare and Scarborough. Countryside areas tend to be protected against massive construction. The National Trust, for example, protects the countryside and coastline from becoming over-commercialized. There are also cultural and historical destinations in the UK. The history of the UK is an attraction to many visitors from overseas. Very popular attractions are called 'honeypots'.

5.10 UK airports and seaports

- UK airports: Travelling to the UK by air is the most common type of travel. London airports have many international flights, and often people transfer there to go to some far away destination as many airports in Europe cannot provide direct flights. Heathrow is often described as a hub airport . When travelling by air, passengers need to be aware of the extra time in the airport, as check-ins and security take time. Airports have a code formed by three letters that are part of the airport's name. For example, LHR stands for London Heathrow. These codes are used for the labels in baggage and tickets.

- UK seaports: The UK has some of busiest ports in Europe. For example, Dover port receives around 16 million people a year.

Dover is the busiest passenger port in the world.

5.20 Road and rail travel

- Road: Within the UK many people travel by road, which can cause traffic jams. Motorways are popular as they allow the driver to go faster than in regular roads. The main North/South motorways are the M1 and the M6. M62 is the main for East/West, and the M5 connects the West Country with the West side. Naturally, coach companies use the motorways although the trip takes longer than with a car due to speed limits for large vehicles.

- Rail: London has many train stations from which trains depart towards many UK destinations all across the country. Each area in the UK is covered by a rail company. For example, there is an East Coast line and a West Coast main line. In Scotland, we find Scotrail, and in North Ireland, Northern Ireland Railways. There is also an international rail line from London to the continent. This is operated by Eurostar.

5.30 Appeal of UK destinations

- Visitor attractions: The UK has a variety of attractions for tourists. London has plenty of places to visit such as historical landmarks, museums, theatres, exhibitions, Westminster Abbey, or the London Eye. Some people like to visit the city itself. Outside London there are some areas such as Brighton on the south coast, Northern England especially near the Pennines, or Scotland, which attracts many tourists who like the natural landscape near Ben Nevis or Loch Ness. Some people might like to spend their stay in the countryside.
- Natural features: These refer to places such as mountains, beaches and coasts, lakes, or rivers. Among all these, National Parks are the most visited.
- Accommodation: There are mainly two kinds of accommodation, 'serviced' and 'unserviced'. The first one includes services such as room cleaning, or breakfast; while the second one does not include them.
- Facilities: These need to be available in the resort or hotel, as tourists might need to stay in if there is bad weather, for example. It is important to keep visitors happy and entertained if they stay in. There are also places such shopping centres which provide many facilities (cinemas, restaurants, etc.) and tourists can also go there. Shopping centres such as Lakeside in Essex, Bluewater in Kent and the Metrocentre in Gateshead in north-east England attract many overseas visitors as well as British ones.
- Arts and entertainment: There are many theatres that offer a wide range of entertainments all across the UK. London's West End theatres are very popular and bring many tourists; the Royal Opera House is another popular venue of higher standard. The Tate Modern, Tate Liverpool, and Tate St Ives also attract many visitors every year. The National Gallery in London is one of the most visited places in London and the UK. During the summer, there are plenty of music festivals, and also theatre and comedy festivals.
- Sightseeing: Tourists like to see all what is possible when they are on holidays. Some cities and towns provide guided tours. There are also ghost tours, for example, the Original Ghost Tour of York. In ghost tours guides with flowing capes tell horror stories to their audiences. There are sightseeing boats in cities such as Canterbury or Glasgow, where there are rivers.
- Transport links: Tourists can take different kinds of public transport such as the tube, trains or buses to move around cities and the country. Usually public transport, such as shuttles, is carefully organised to facilitate mobility to travellers. Opting for public transport also avoids more traffic jams and reduces generally carbon emissions.

5.40 Increasing appeal of the UK tourism sector

- Improving facilities: As the tourism sector is generally very competent and many overseas visitors make a conscious choice about their country of destination, it is important for the holiday resorts, hotels, and attractions to keep improving their services and facilities. For example, resorts or camping areas might decide to include a swimming pool or a children's area. Museums, for example, can become more attractive to visitors by including interactive activities, or having some didactic areas for children. Theme parks can include more live shows; for example, at Halloween they can perform a horror show.

- Appealing to specific groups: Visitors who do not speak English will feel discouraged to come to the UK if they suspect they will struggle to communicate. To avoid this staff should learn some languages in order to make visitors feel welcome. Tour guides might need to speak foreign languages particularly well. Written information needs to be in many languages as well. Regarding visitors with disabilities, attractions should try to adapt their facilities. For example, including wheelchair ramps.

5.50 Sources of information

- Paper-based sources: These include guidebooks, maps, leaflets, brochures and any kind of printed material. Many tourism information offices give free leaflets with information on the main attractions to visitors. The problem with paper-based sources is that they need to be reprinted often in order to being updated, and this costs more money.
- Online resources: These tend to be more updated but you need to be careful about the websites you find, as some might belong to private companies trying to sell their products, and be more impartial about the information provided. It is better to visit official websites such as council sites. VisitBritain is the UK's official tourism website.
- Bibliography: If your organisation gives information to customers you need to state the source of information, for example, at the end of the leaflet you provide.

5.60 To know more: British railway system

In recent years, many railway operators have become more market oriented, this applied even before the privatisation of British rail from 1994 onwards.

The supply of railways was affected in the UK by many factors. For example, a number of lines in the United Kingdom were reduced because of the Beeching report in 1963. Some of these cuts have been reversed and sometimes heritage railways have also come into being: they run around 500 miles of track, attracting a large number of different tourists.

Trains can become very busy during peak times, particularly trains via London. (Marylebone station)

There are a number of different private operators in the United Kingdom. They include Virgin trains, SNCF, Spoorwegen, part of the Chinese nationalised railways, also Deutscher Bahn.

There has been more emphasis on transferring fuel from diesel to electric but there are concerns about the spiralling costs of some of the electrification plans. Since December 2016, more emphasis has been placed on moving away from Network Rail to having integrated services between the operators and stations.

The demand for railways will vary tremendously between peak and off-peak times. During the holiday periods, many trains in France get very crowded but the introduction of the TGV trains which are very high-speed, means that they can carry much larger numbers than would have been possible with conventional trains. The TGV services are being extended both within France and to the neighbouring countries, including Italy and Spain.

Many of the European railway services have had sleeper trains and couchettes. This is very helpful to many people who like the idea of avoiding looking around for accommodation.

There is also a considerable demand, particularly in the UK, for what is sometimes called the nostalgic market.

There is considerable price differentiation and discrimination. The railway operators in the UK, for example, have cards for senior citizens (60+), family card, as well as a student card and a disabled card all of which may affect the demand for the railway services. The advantage of the disabled card is that it is available all the time and that a disabled person can always have one other person with them for the same reduced fare. The concept of disabled is much wider than many people would assume, since it includes people who have been prescribed NHS hearing aids as well as the visually and mentally handicapped. For the first time since privatisation in 1994, a new Railcard has been introduced, this is called 'two together'. Any two people who regularly travel can use this card which cost £30 a year in early 2017.

5.70 Inter-rail

Inter-rail is a cooperation between different parts of the European rail system and provides deals for young people under the age of 26. There are similar packages for older people that cost slightly more. Inter-rail tickets are cheap compared with the cost of individual journeys, and many young people like them because it gives them a very worthwhile experience. The following were the prices in 2016:

Global InterRail pass prices 2016	2nd class InterRail	
	Adult (aged 26-59)	Youth (under 26)
5 days in 15 days (flexi)	£205	£154
7 days in 1 month (flexi)	£245	£189
10 days in 1 month (flexi)	£289	£221

When British Railways was still nationalised, concern developed around golden rail holidays, and the assumption was that many people would like to be able to use the railways as part of the holiday experience rather than having to travel by car where they could be held up in traffic jams. The railways subsequently from the Channel Tunnel, which was first opened in 1994, found that many people liked to travel to and from Europe. However, when the original forecast was made the assumption was about 20,000,000 journeys would be made a year whereas the total number of journeys was around 7 million when it first opened. However, this has gradually risen to around 20,000,000 journeys a year.

Some people suffer from seasickness, and they will be grateful to be able to use rail services as part of their journeys.

The heritage railway has also been part of the enjoyment for many people which might be considered part of the nostalgic market.

Michael Portillo, the former Conservative cabinet minister, has presented many programmes on BBC about both British and continental travel. In turn, this may well have had the effect of encouraging follow in his steps.

5.80 To know more: Coach Companies

From London Victoria Coach Station, there are many express services to and from European destinations. Outside London, Cheltenham is often a convenient interchange for many people. Coach services are often one of the cheapest forms of transport and therefore coach operators can compete on price. Whilst in the United Kingdom there are maximum speed limits on coaches, which are lower than the rail, sometimes the greater number of destinations served means that accessibility time is less. There are hour restrictions on bus and coach drivers which have increased costs for operators. However, this will have also improved safety. This is important to the industry as there is much more publicity in the media about coach crashes which are comparatively rare than publicity to people being killed in car accidents where the number of people killed is still around 1,500 per year in the United Kingdom.

5.90 To know more: tourism destinations

The tourism industry has grown partly because of political factors. For example, the breakup of the Soviet Union around 1989 to 1991 encouraged more Eastern Europeans to travel to areas where they were not previously allowed to go. The ending of the apartheid era in South Africa from 1995 meant that more people were willing to travel to and from that country. The increase in the number of countries within the European Union to 28 from 2013 meant that it was much easier for people to travel within these countries. Other regional groupings such as the Association of Southeastern Asian Nations (ASEAN) will have had similar effects. ASEAN is comprised of 10 member states: Thailand, Vietnam, Laos, Cambodia, Brunei, Myanmar (Burma), Singapore, Indonesia, Malaysia and the Philippines.

Many people have been killed in the Syrian civil war since the Arab Spring of 2012, and the impact of this will be to deter people from travelling to the Middle East region. Similarly, the attacks on the Tunisian coast in 2015 have been widely publicised and many beaches are currently deserted.

There are many travel programmes on television which mean that people are much more aware of what is happening in other countries and the potential opportunities. Penelope Keith a well-known TV actress has hosted some tourist programmes on television and so have Prunella Scales another well-known TV actress and her husband Timothy West. John Sargent, the former BBC chief diplomatic correspondent, has also visited many places and this will have made them better known.

Apart from the travel programmes, many people will also have seen on both news and other programmes details about the ways in which other people live and therefore may want to explore the changes in cuisine and culture which tourism can often offer.

The increase in the number of middle class people in India and China will have added to the number of people wishing to travel to other countries. The total number and the amount they have spent in the United Kingdom will be available from the Office for National Statistics (ONS).

5.100 Higher incomes

Higher incomes in many Western countries before the credit crunch 2007 will also have affected demand for travel and tourism. There is a strong correlation between incomes and demand for tourism. Within the UK, the Office for National Statistics provides many sources of data which both students and tourist operators will be interested in.

5.110 Effect of improved transport infrastructure and other transport improvements

The channel tunnel opened in 1994 and the road and rail bridge between Denmark-Sweden (connected by Oresund Bridge and under water tunnel) has offered new opportunities for many people to travel more easily between different countries.

Air travel costs have come down significantly with newer budget airlines such as EasyJet offering very cheap flights. The budget airlines have made considerable inroads into the aviation market and have also opened up new routes which led to more opportunities for travel. However, because of grandfather rights at Heathrow airport it is often difficult for the newer airlines be able to give accessibility to London. Some of the newer airlines will be able to use City airport in the Docklands area of London.

Disneyland Florida and Disneyland Paris will have enticed more people to travel to these attractions. Eurostar currently runs trains directly from London to Disneyland in France which makes it easy for potential travellers to get there. Theme parks at Alton Towers and Chessington in Surrey are also popular destinations for many people particularly these with children. The railway runs very near to Chessington Station and is therefore readily accessible to London by rail. Older people using the freedom pass which is available after the morning peak can travel directly to Chessington by either bus or train free of charge.

The National Trust often provides sheets for children to fill in so that they look for different hidden items which they may take delight in searching for. The logic behind this is that not only will more visitors come but also that they will stay longer and buy more items. Also, habit is an important determinant of demand and if children are used to visiting National Trust places they will be more inclined to become members when they are older.

Similarly, London museums such as the Science Museum have always attracted many visitors of all ages but often have special exhibitions which are of particular interest to different tourists. The Natural History Museum is also very popular.

Whilst cathedrals and other places of worship have their main objective as persuading people to worship, they are often major tourist attractions and often guides take visitors around the buildings showing them features which they might not otherwise have observed. Sometimes places will be regarded as sacred and Iona off the west coast of Scotland attracts a number of visitors. Similarly, Holy Island in Northumbria attracts tourists for both day trips and longer periods.

Sometimes churches and abbeys have been converted into secular buildings such as is the case with Combermere Abbey in Shropshire where the north wing was changed in the 16th century to become a mansion, and then again in the 19th century to a more Gothic format. Visitors over 16 can use the accommodation for bed and breakfast.

Many abbeys were destroyed on the orders of Henry VIII, and Thomas Cromwell, a distant relative of Oliver Cromwell, gave detailed instructions on how this should be carried out. Oliver Cromwell, who was the MP for Ely, now has a Museum named after him in Ely, and visitors can vote as to whether he was a devil or a hero.

The Taj Mahal in India, which was built by one of the Mogul rulers to commemorate his beloved wife, is a place which many people will want to visit. (More cynical people might notice that she was one of his eight wives and he also had a large number of concubines).

The Great Wall of China is often said to be one of the few man-made objects which can be seen from space and whilst for many years many foreigners would not have been allowed to go near the wall it is now a major attraction for many people, and although there are some concerns about damage to the wall it is a major tourist attraction.

Hadrian's Wall, which marked the Roman boundary between the Roman Empire and the Picts, has been heavily marketed as a place to visit and there is a bus service bearing the number AD 122 which runs across the border. The number A.D. 122 is the date when Hadrian, Roman emperor from AD 76-AD138, started to build the wall. Scotland was never part of the Roman Empire. The bus service is a convenient way of getting near the wall which will be of interest to some visitors.

SCUBA diving enables people to visit places under the sea which are often less well-known than many other places. They will therefore attract people who like novelty and are adventurous.

Similarly, the Cutty Sark was one of the fastest clippers when the first tea of the season could arrive in England and would command a higher price than later tea. It is now situated in Greenwich near the National Maritime Museum in south-east London. It has been extensively repaired after a fire in 2014, and is now a major attraction for tourists. One of the stations nearby is called Cutty Sark and is on the Docklands Light Railway which offers a very frequent service.

Similarly, the Mary Rose, which was Henry VIII's flagship at the time when the English king was busy fighting against Roman Catholic countries such as Spain and France, has been conserved and is now a major attraction in Portsmouth in Hampshire. It was called Mary Rose as a tribute to his sister and had been built in 1509 in the year when he came to the throne in England. It sank in 1545 when the French arrived in the Isle of Wight. It is of interest to many people because of the artefacts which have been unearthed since that time.

Vasa (or Wasa) is a Swedish warship built between 1626 and 1628. The ship foundered after sailing about 1,300 m (1,400 yd) into her maiden voyage on 10 August 1628. People knew that the ship was unstable but dared not tell the Swedish king that it was. It is now a major tourist attraction in Sweden.

SS Great Britain, which was the steamship built by the well-known engineer Isambard Kingdom Brunel, was brought back to Bristol having been scuppered near the Falkland Islands off South America, and has been painstakingly restored. It now forms another major attraction.

In Northern Ireland, the SS Titanic was launched by Harland and Wolff in 1912 in Belfast. It was a luxury liner where sufficient detail had not been paid to safety and not enough lifeboats had been installed on her. It was about 400 miles from the Newfoundland coast when it hit an iceberg and sank on its maiden voyage. It has become even more famous recently because of the film Titanic in 1997 starring Leonardo di Caprio and Kate Winslet. In spite of the tragedy killing 1517 people, the Titanic Museum has now become a major attraction in Northern Ireland.

The Giants Causeway between Northern Ireland and the Scottish mainland is a protected UNESCO site, one of the few in the United Kingdom and many people go there every year. There are a number of legends about the Giants Causeway and the attraction gives details of some of these.

The first recorded ascent of Mount Everest was in May 1953 by Sir Edmund Hillary and his companion Tenzing Norgay just before Queen Elizabeth the Second's coronation on June 2, 1953. Many other people now wish to climb Everest and it is a major tourist attraction for people visiting Nepal.

Not everyone can be so adventurous but it is possible to visit the Norwegian fjords much more easily and play. Many visitors can go on day trips to the Fjords called Norway in a nutshell.

Many people also use the steam train which goes from near Carnarvon to the top of Snowdon which is Wales's highest peak.

The Ffestiniog and Welsh Highland Railway now offers the longest regular steam train ride in Wales. It goes from near Caernarvon near the North coast of Wales, which offers splendid views of Snowdonia, to Porthmadog on the West Welsh coast. Many tourists enjoy it as a novelty and in an area where there are few roads, which can become very congested in the summer. It offers both an interesting scenic journey and also an interesting variety of small stations to stop at on route if people wish to do so.

Many tourists also enjoy the more relaxed atmosphere of the railway which is run mainly by volunteers and where staff will be willing to talk to passengers if they so wish.

The National Railway Museum at York is very near York station and so therefore accessible to many people. The museum itself runs onto many railway lines so that the exhibits can often be used which creates another tourist attraction.

The Mallard, which holds the world record for a steam train at 126 mph, has been used to haul trains from York. The recently reopened Waverley line from Edinburgh to the border towns such as Galashiels in Scotland. The Scottish government led by Nicola Sturgeon also helped to create more publicity. It is hoped that the railway line will eventually go further to Carlisle.

The Keighley and Worth railway was used during the filming of the original Railway Children film in 1970 starring amongst others Jenny Agutter and Lionel Jeffries. It has used this publicity at some of its stations between Keighley and Oxenhope to generate more tourist traffic.

6. International Tourism Destinations I: Europe

In this chapter, we will define Europe as the whole of the continent from the Urals and Ireland to the Canary Islands, the Azores and Cyprus. The most common holidays in Europe are short city breaks, or longer holidays in the Mediterranean or mountain areas. In winter, skiing resorts such as these found in the Pyrenees and the Alps are common destinations.

The Aurora Borealis (Northern Lights) draw tourists to Iceland during the winter months.

6.10 Holiday destinations

- Summer: In summer, the Mediterranean countries are the most common destinations. Spain, Italy, Greece, and France are very popular destinations, where food and drink is often cheaper; there is also a lively nightlife, and other entertainments such as golf clubs.
- Winter: If your customer is looking for winter sun you can advise on a trip to Malta, Madeira, or the Canary Islands. It will not be as warm as in summer, and the sea might be slightly colder but the weather remains sunny overall. For customers looking for winter sports, there are many ski resorts where different activities are offered: after skiing you can enjoy music, drinks, or sleigh riding. The most common locations for ski resorts are the Alps across Italy, France, Switzerland, Austria, and Slovenia, and the Pyrenees between France and Spain.
- Countryside areas: In summer, some customers look for a bit of fresh air and decide to go to the countryside. Hiking trails and sporting activities are common offers from countryside areas. Water sports are available in valleys and lakes.
- City breaks: Cities are a good option for people looking for cultural and heritage activities.
- Cruise areas: Cruises can take different routes. For example, one might start a cruise in the English Channel and end in the Mediterranean, or one could fly to a Mediterranean port and start there. There are also Baltic cruises, in which you can visit, for example, Russian cities. Nowadays there are low-cost cruises with easyCruise.

6.20 European gateways

- Airports: European capital cities have at least one airport, and smaller cities without airports have very good connections to the nearby airport. With the introduction of Ryanair many minor cities have been allocated an airport, as Ryanair usually flies to airports further away from capital cities.
- Passenger ferry ports: Access to Europe is also possible by ferry.
- Channel tunnel: You can access the continent by car, train, or bus through the channel. The channel starts in Folkestone and arrives at Calais Fréthun. The cars, however, travel in drive-on/drive-off carriages while the passengers stay inside.
- Eurostar terminals: These are in London St. Pancras, Ebbsfleet International, and Ashford International. From these terminals, you can arrive or depart to Brussels and Paris.
- Travel and transfer times: When planning a trip, it is important to make sure that the customer will arrive at the final destination. You need to organise all the transfers necessary, and be especially careful if the customer is travelling to a remote destination with difficult access.

6.30 Types of destination

- Natural features: There are four main kinds of natural features in Europe: mountains, lakes and rivers, forests and woods, and beaches. The highest mountains in Europe are the Pyrenees and Alps. In these there are many facilities such as skiing resorts, walking, and climbing. Walking, together with water sports, is also part of lake

Mont Blanc is the tallest mountain in Europe.

and rivers resorts. In the French lake Dordogne, it is possible to do rafting, while bigger rivers, such as the Rhine, even have cruisers. In forests and woods, you can go cycling and riding. Some tourists like to feel removed from civilization, and enjoy living in nature. They can book a hut or cottage to stay in. Finally, beaches are known for being beautiful spots. There are many types of beaches: from rocky to sandy beaches, large public ones, or small coves; beaches on the Atlantic, the Mediterranean, or the Adriatic side.

- Local attractions: Historical sites, museums, and theme parks are the most common local attractions. There are, for example, pre-historic caves and monuments in France and Spain. Italy is, for example, rich in Roman and Renaissance architecture, and of course, Greece presents many Antique sites. There are many World Heritage Sites in Europe; Croatia, for example, has whole towns which are considered Heritage Sites. Museums are rich in works of art. The most important museums are the Louvre in Paris, or the Prado in Madrid. Theme parks are meant to be fun both for children and adults. They present many attractions and shows. Parks such as Disneyland Paris, Port Aventura in Spain, or Efterling in the Netherlands are some examples.

Lascaux Cave Painting

6.40 Range of accommodation

As seen in previous chapters, you need to be careful to help your customer choose the best accommodation option. Remember that there are different types of accommodation in price, architectural type, and in relation to the facilities they provide.

6.50 Facilities

- Local transport: Once in the country of destination, tourists get around by walking or with public transport. Taking the tram, for example, in many European cities can be a nice experience, and part of enjoying the new country. There are also bikes available, or horse carriages for a more folkloric experience.

- Shopping: This can also be a very local experience. People can go to local markets and buy local food, which they cannot usually find in their countries. Some goods are cheaper in some countries than in others.

- Nightlife: Some customers are very interested in nightlife, and they will look for a destination with a known nightlife. Clubbing, concerts, and discos might be sought after for such tourists. Other more sophisticated evening activities, such as theatre and opera, are also on offer. Vienna, for example, has more of a cultural nightlife than Ibiza or Berlin, where cheap clubbing and disco are more common.

- Sport and leisure: Sport can be the reason for travelling to a destination. Your customer/s might wish to attend a match, or bigger events such as the Olympics or Paralympics0 , or the World Cup. Other customers might prefer to do sport themselves, and look for locations where to play golf, adventure, or water sports.

6.60 Traditions and cultural aspects

It is part of your responsibility to make sure that your customer knows about the differences in culture and religion of the country of destination. Some countries, especially in Eastern Europe, are more conservative, and it is not permitted to 'binge-drink', for example. A tourist can be arrested for being drunk. In some countries, it is considered offensive for a young couple to sleep together before marriage, or for women to go inappropriately dressed, especially in Islamic countries. At religious sites, both men and women need to follow a dress code.

6.70 Climate

The weather can be one of the reasons for travelling. Usually people in the UK wish to visit warmer countries with longer sunlight hours. The climate in a country depends on:

- Its distance from the equator: temperature is less variable if a country is near the equator.
- Its distance from the oceans: being far away from the oceans makes the temperature more extreme.
- Altitude: if the country is higher above the sea, the cooler it is.
- Wind: in windy areas temperatures are more moderate.

People travelling should be made aware of areas where natural disasters can occur. Earthquakes, droughts, and floods should be avoided, as well as extreme temperatures in winter and summer.

7. International destinations II: Worldwide holidays

7.10 Destinations
Worldwide destinations allow the customer to choose among many options and kinds of holidays. There are often three main kinds of destination:

- Towns and cities: These are perfect for shopping holidays, entertainment, sightseeing, or cultural travelling.
- Beach resorts: These vary from very luxurious and quiet paradises to party spots.
- Islands: There are many types of islands. Some are known for their coasts and others for their countryside, or maybe both. Islands also might have nice towns to visit.

Destinations can also be classified into these known for their natural significance (natural parks, or safaris, for example) and these known for their historical significance (Greek and Roman ruins).

UNESCO World Heritage sites, such as Toledo in Spain, are prime destinations for tourists who seek sites of culture and natural beauty.

7.20 Different types of holiday
- History and culture: Some people travel because they are interested in foreign cultures, or ancient civilisations. History and culture usually go together. Some activities people look for are related to historical and cultural amenities, as tourists often like to experience local music, art, traditional dances and food, religion.
- Beach relaxation: Some people like going too far away destinations, such as the Caribbean, to enjoy beach relaxation and a nice weather. Some of these destinations also offer aquatic activities such as surfing (in Australia, for example), and scuba diving. The Maldives, for example, would be an example of luxury, offering tranquil and idyllic locations and accommodation. It is very common for honeymoons. Other beach resorts, such as Goa in

India, are more popular among backpackers as they can find hostels for long stays, beach bars and restaurants.

- Weddings and honeymoons: Usually couples and their families spend large amounts of money on their honeymoon. Some even marry in exotic destinations (beach weddings) where they will also spend the honeymoon. The arrangements for these kinds of wedding are usually made by the resort itself or tour operators, which offer tailor-made wedding holidays. Everything, including the paper work is organised. Many hotels have special offers for honeymooners such as free champagne or flowers, or maybe a free spa treatment.
- Leisure and entertainment: Some of the most popular leisure destinations are the Disneyland resorts around the world. The most popular of these is the one in Florida. There are other examples of entertainment such as Las Vegas, Broadway, or Universal Studios.
- Winter sports: There are many sport possibilities beyond Europe. Canada, for example, is a good destination for snow sports.
- Natural world: Some people like to be surrounded by nature and see marvellous landscapes. Maybe they are looking for adventure sports. Typical activities to do in a natural or wild environment are safaris, or trekking holidays. People can also have guided tours in the desert, or jungles.

Outdoor activities can combine sports and outstanding natural beauty.

- Adventure: Usually adventure travelling takes place in the natural world, as it is associated with activities such as trekking, scuba diving, or rafting.

7.30 Types of customers

- Couples: They might plan on travelling to a faraway destination for special occasions, or just for the pleasure of enjoying romantic or exotic holidays. Many people celebrate golden, silver or ruby wedding anniversaries by visiting a worldwide destination.
- Singles: This type of customer might enjoy destinations with lots of activities to meet new people; or they might enjoy relaxing on their own.
- Families: In helping families to organise their holidays one needs to consider the children's age. If the family travels with a baby, destinations with mild temperatures might be more appropriate. Also, the locations should be appropriate, for example, quiet towns are better than busy cities. There are also family-friendly accommodations. If the children were older it would be good to look for places with activities for children, or safety places.
- Groups: Some customers travel in groups. They might wish to go skiing together, or to perform some other adventure activities. Party holidays, such as Ibiza, are also sought-after groups, especially of young people. End of school trips might like to go to a worldwide destination as well. Other groups can be students in their gap year, or retired people. These groups will have very different needs and tastes you need to address.

7.40 Foreign and Commonwealth Office (FCO)

The FCO is a government department whose work is to inform British travelling abroad about safety, weather, and healthy issues. Information is available on FCO's website. It is good to visit the webpage when travelling to remote and less well-known destinations.

7.50 Extreme weather

Flooding is more likely to occur during the monsoon.

In some countries, you need to be aware of extreme weather conditions as weather can lead to life threatening situations. There are phenomena such as the monsoon season and tropical storms. The monsoon season causes torrential downpours that lead to flooding and travel disruptions. This happens in India mostly, and sometimes in Australia, America, and East Asia. Tropical storms vary from being very windy to hurricanes. Some seasons are riskier than others, and if travelling in a hurricane area, it is good to check when it is the best time to go in order to avoid encountering extreme storms. If the weather is not dangerous, it is still worth checking as the customer might be expecting sunny days and find rain.

7.60 Health issues

- Pandemics: This happens when an infectious disease has spread in such a degree that exceeds epidemic proportions. A pandemic moves across countries, and it can even affect the whole world. Examples of pandemics are the bird flu (2005), the swine flu (2009). People are advised to not to travel in areas at risk.
- Malaria: It is an infectious disease transmitted through mosquitoes. You can be contaminated with Malaria in hot and humid countries such as parts of Africa and Asia. There are preventive measures against malaria.

7.70 Safety

- Crime: Some countries have higher crime rates than others. In general, tourists are easy targets for pickpockets as travellers are less familiar with the area, and tend to be more distracted with sightseeing. Some parts of the world, however, are especially dangerous; for example, in many parts of Central America, where violent crimes take place.
- Terrorism: Anywhere can be a target of a terrorist attack but some areas are more at risk than others.
- Unrest: Revolts against the government can lead to riots, strikes, and in extreme cases, civil wars. Tourists can find themselves caught in some of these situations, which can be very frightening. The FCO also reports these kinds of events.

7.80 Social conditions

People travelling to third world countries should know that they will see extreme poverty and hardship. Seeing poverty can be uncomfortable. In some countries beggars surround tourists nearby their hotels. Tourists may probably see children in miserable conditions too, and this is even a more extreme experience.

7.90 Entry and exit requirements

- Visas: This is a permit issued by a country, and it allows you to stay, work, or study in that country. In some countries entry is not possible without a visa. You should be aware of the visa requirements for your customers, and be updated in each of the countries' requirements. This information can be found in the embassies.
- Vaccination certificates: Some countries require a yellow fever vaccination certificate. Yellow fever is a deadly disease transmitted by mosquitoes. The tropical parts of Asia and South America are dangerous in these regards. Travellers must check in advance (around 6 weeks before departure) the travelling requirements as medical treatments can take time.
- Departure tax: Many countries in Latin America, Asia and Africa have a departure tax that tourists need to pay when leaving the country. These taxes can be included in the flight ticket, or you might need to pay them in cash in the airport. They can be over £100.

7.100 World economy

- Recession: It takes place when there is an economic slump. It usually brings unemployment. During a recession people spend their money more carefully, and they might look for shorter, or more economical, holidays. Holiday providers, such as hotel resorts, might put on offers.
- Exchange rates: Depending on how high a currency is against the pound sterling; some travellers might feel more inclined to visit some countries rather than others. If the currency of the country of destination is low, British travellers will find it cheaper, it will be easier to stay in a better hotel. One factor which we have not yet mentioned, which may well help individuals to decide where to go on holiday, is exchange rates. For example, when £1 was worth about $1.33 at the time of the 2016 referendum in the UK, a $2,000 holiday in the U.S.A. would have cost about £1503. A similar holiday costing $2,000 at a rate of $1.27 = £1 (which was about the rate in December 2016) would cost about £1,574, making a visit to the U.S.A. less attractive but making a trip to the U.K. for American tourists more attractive. The drop in the value of sterling following the European Union referendum will have made it much cheaper for American tourists to visit the United Kingdom. It is not however just the cost of travel to and from a country which will affect the demand but also the price of goods and services within the country. Some other countries have had much more violent fluctuations in their currency so the effect will be much greater than in the example above. The large tourism operators as well as shipping companies and other transport organisations will often use the forward exchange currency markets. This means that they can buy currency now at a fixed rate which avoids the sharp changes in currency. This would particularly apply to countries such as Malawi and Zimbabwe.

8. Marketing in Tourism

8.10 Definition

Marketing consists of promoting your products to potential customers. For this, you need to first  identify who is a potential customer. Targeting the right audience is key to successful marketing. You also need to think about a right price for your products, and when it is the best moment to promote them. Finally, you need to address the most important question in marketing: how will I promote my products? For a good marketing strategy, you might need to do some market research. This involves asking your potential customers what they expect, for example, from a travel agency. Being aware of customer needs is crucial for marketing.

8.20 Function of marketing

It is important to realise that marketing is not only about advertising but also about dealing with promotion and evaluation, product development, and knowing customer needs. Important points in marketing are the following:

- First of all, you should start identifying customer needs. It is very helpful to ask them whether they liked the holidays, the services they bought from you, what would they improve? And why? Personal characteristics such as age, gender, hobbies and interests are of help in determining what a customer would like.
- Secondly, once you have become familiar with the customer's needs and tastes you will develop the product and services which you think the customer wishes. To develop a successful product, you need to consider budget, location, and features.
- The next step consists in finding the right way to promote your product. Ways of advertising are direct mail, sponsorship, ads, among others that we will study in the following pages.
- Finally, you need to evaluate the whole marketing process and be aware that this might need to change or adapt to new needs.

8.30 Marketing mix

Marketing mix, also called 4Ps, is formed by the four most important factors: product, price, place and promotion. The balance between these factors is key to successful marketing. However, this balance is different for everyone: a new company might need to focus on making itself known, therefore, by promotion; while an established company might need to focus on prices and products to be competitive in the market and ensure customers return.

8.40 Marketing segmentation

This is a process which consists in dividing the total market for a product or service into different segments. Segmentation helps to focus on the needs of each group of customers (customers who want similar things). Markets can be segmented as follows:

- Region: people living in a particular area could be target for a holiday brochure. This group of people might share a similar wealth, and have a similar budget when it comes to holiday bookings.
- Age: that would imply designing holiday products for age groups, for example, 18-25, or over 60.
- Social class: targeting people in a particular area which is defined by a social class.
  group: you can focus on holidays for women or men.
- Life style: some people like adventure, and you could design an adventure product.

8.50 Marketing communication methods

The 7 Ps of Services Marketing

To communicate with your customer, you can use a range of methods besides advertising, such as print items, direct marketing, public relations work, sales promotion and sponsorship. The main purpose of communication is to inform customers about your products, and sell them.

8.60 E-marketing

This includes internet advertising, text messaging, and e-mail marketing. E-marketing is growing fastest within the field of marketing. E-marketing effectively targets customers. Internet advertisement has also the advantage of being very cheap.

8.70 Factors influencing marketing in travel and tourism
- Company ethos: marketing must conform to ethical and moral standards. Showing racial or sexual prejudices does not conform to such standards. All companies need to show social

responsibility. For example, some companies agree to the principles of "green tourism". That means that they promote holidays that do not impact negatively on the environment.

- Consumer protection: The Consumer Protection Act 1987 makes it a criminal offence to give misleading information about prices. Therefore, the tourism operators must ensure that the prices shown in brochures, for example, are correct. The Trades Description Act 1968 protects customers against false descriptions given by suppliers of goods and services. The Data Protection Act 1998 ensures high standards of discretion when companies deal with personal information from their customers.
- Standards of practice: this describes voluntary codes of practice, for example, the Association of British Travel Agents (ABTA) Code of Conduct. Such codes of practice provide guidelines on how to behave in case of incident; for example, complaints procedures or compensation payments. Advertising is also regulated by Advertising Standards Authority (ASA) which regulates advertising in all media.
- Political, economic, social and technological (PEST) factors: some external factors can affect tourism marketing, and companies do not have control over them. PEST analysis is a technique to analyse the external factors, and it includes political (e.g. European Union policy on travel), economic (e.g. exchange rates), social (e.g. lifestyle changes), and technological information (e.g. payment methods).

8.80 Product

Tourism products can be sold separately. For example, you can book a hotel room, or you can buy a whole package including a hotel room, flight, and car hire. Tourism products can be: short breaks, airline flights, tourist attractions, car hire, coach travel, package holidays, hotel accommodation, and cruises. Travel and tourism products are intangible, perishable, and service-related. That means that you cannot touch or grasp them in the same way you can, for example, with a mobile phone. Perishable refers to the fact that the good can devalue from one day to the next; therefore, it is a lost for the company. Finally, employees in the travel industry deal mostly with customers, and employees need to stand to the standards.

8.90 Characteristics of products

- Branding: Companies spend an important amount of time in branding. A clear brand gives customers an identifiable name or logo, and it is important because people will become familiar with it. If customers have a good experience with a brand they will most likely come back. The brand is identifiable in staff uniforms, for example, or stationery.
- USPs: This stands for Unique Selling Proposition. It means that a product or service has a special benefit over another one. For example, the USP for a hotel might be that it provides a discount for honeymoon suites.
- Product life cycle: nearly all goods and services have a lifespan as products and services become fashionable and at some point, they stop being so. For this reason, products and services need to be rethought and redesigned, or you can also create new products. The life cycle of a product is formed of five stages: Launch (the product is launched, and a lot of money is spent on promotion); growth (sales grow and profit increases); maturity (sales tend to stabilize, and the company needs to decide if it should remove the product from the market or redesign it); saturation (sales reach a maximum); and decline (profits fall).

8.100 Price

It is important to have the right price; otherwise, promotion will not help to sell the product. There are five main factors which influence the product. These are:

- Costs: The organisation needs to know the expenses of providing a particular service in order to price it correctly. The service or product should not be too expensive but it should provide a profit to the company.
- Seasonality: Prices change depending on the demand. They can change through the seasons and even through the day. For example, demand for holiday increases in the months of July and August in the northern hemisphere, and prices are more expensive in these months than in September. Flight tickets might be cheaper very early in the morning or late at night.
- Competitor activity: An organisation needs to be aware of the competitor's activities and adjust prices accordingly. If the competitor offers the same service quality for a lower price, it is likely to get more customers than another company with higher prices.
- The state of the economy: If there is a recession, for example, prices might be lowered as the alternative may result in the product not being sold.
- Objectives of the organisation: A private company might need to maximize benefits, and that would be the objective when thinking about the prices of its products. Conversely, a non-profit organisation would guarantee more affordable prices in order to focus on their social aims.

In pricing, there are a series of pricing strategies, such as the following:

- Skimming: This takes place when a high price is charged for a new exclusive product. The pricing of luxury hotels is an example of skimming.
- Cost-plus pricing: This is the total cost of fixed and variable costs. On the top of these, there is an addition which is the profit made.
- Penetration pricing: This is used by organisations which wish to introduce a product that is already offered by other companies. In this case, the price is lower.
- Competitive pricing: This means that a product sold by different organisations will be sold at the same price in all cases.
- Variable pricing: This applies when a product changes price during the day, season, or by any other reasons.

8.110 Place

Place regarding marketing refers to location and accessibility as well as the way in which products are made available to customers – this is known as channels of distribution. Location and accessibility are very important for the success of a tourism product. Some remote products, for instance, a guest house in the countryside, might be difficult to access, therefore the owner would need to ensure good communication. Accessibility also applies to, for example, customers with disabilities. Facilities need to ensure people with disabilities can access the premises. Internet is the most used channel by users who look for holidays.

8.120 Promotion

Promotions aim at the following:

- Making the products known to customers.
- Informing customers about the benefits of the products.
- Trying to increase demand for products.
- Incentivising the purchase of products.
- Reminding customers of the products.

The budget spent in promotion varies from company to company. It depends on the aims of the organisation (the types of products that they sell, and to whom). There are six main types of promotion methods:

- Advertising: This can be advertising in the press, which is the most common media for advertising, and high amounts are spent on it. Newspapers and magazines can be relatively cheap to advertise in, depending on the publication. Messages can be sent locally, regionally, or nationally. Through the choice of the press, specific segments of the market are targeted. Adverts can be placed at short notice. The second most important form of advertising is through social media and television. Advertising on TV can be expensive but it is particularly effective. TV advertising reaches large audiences and it can be very creative; the message is also more dynamic, and the advertisement can be repeated. Commercial radio advertising is very useful for local and regional advertisements. Radio advertisement is one of the cheapest media for advertising, and the message can be repeated on TV. Cinema advertising would be more suitable for products aimed at youth, or high-income people; the costs though are high. Cinema advertising is also a kind of local advertising. Finally, outdoor and transport advertising can be anything from trains and buses to sport ground advertising.
- Public relations: The main activity for PR is to keep the media informed about the organisations' updates. However, PR refers to any kind of contact with the public from reception to calls.
- Sales promotions: The main kind of sale promotion techniques are discount vouchers, price cuts, extra products (e.g. 2 for the price of 1), free gifts, prize draws, competitions, free stationery, free membership, and displays and exhibitions. The main different between advertising and sales promotion is that this last one aims at selling in the short term.
- Direct marketing: This can target particular types of people directly. Direct mail, for example, is used for direct marketing. In the mail, potential customers can be addressed by their names.
- Internet marketing: This is very cheap and flexible. This kind of advertising is growing as people use the Internet a lot.
- Print materials: These refer to items such as brochures and leaflets. They are used to sell a large variety of products from hotels to tours. Holiday brochures have the following purposes: accurately presenting products and services to potential customers, conveying an image of the company, converting an inquiry into a sale, offering a means to book a holiday, explaining booking and contractual conditions, and presenting the information within the legal UK and EU bonds.

9. Market research

why?
who?
how?
WHEN?
Where?

Market research is an activity performed by companies and organisations in order to know who their target audiences are, and how to develop more successful products for them.

9.10 Planning

A research activity should follow a planned process. We suggest you follow the following steps:

- Identify objectives: These are the goals an organisation sets itself. Some examples could be to increase profitability by reducing costs by 7% in the next year and a half; challenge the opposition by developing a new product; build the company's image by increasing the amount of stationery; increase market share by capturing another 8% of the total sales, enter new markets by increasing the number of holiday destinations; and combining elements of the marketing mix by spending more budget on promotion and less on distribution. The objectives a company sets itself should be SMART (specific, measurable, achievable, realistic, and timed).
- Plan research methods: There are two kind of research methods, which are those included in primary research and in secondary research. Primary research collects data that is not available from any other available source. Secondary research analyses data that is already available. There are three forms of primary research methods; these are surveys, observations, and focus groups:

1. Surveys are often used to collect primary data. There are four main types of surveys, which are face-to-face interview survey, self-completed questionnaire survey, telephone survey, and email survey. In a face-to-face interview survey, we ask a series of questions to a member of the public. In this kind of interview, the interviewer can explain difficult questions, as well as ask more detail from the respondent (interviewed). However face-to-face interviews can be very expensive because you need to hire and train interviewers. A self-completed survey is a questionnaire without the need for an interviewer. This method is cheaper than a face-to-face interview, and questionnaires can be found in the exit doors of attractions in order to know the opinion of the customers. Telephone and email surveys are economical survey methods, and they can also be fast. However, some people might not like the idea of receiving a phone call in order to fill a questionnaire.

2. Observation: Your organisation might also observe the competitor's products. Observers might be discreet and be mixed with the general public in order to hide themselves from the competence. By being among the general public, they can observe how a product performs (strengths and weakness) in order to then create a better one. Observation can also give information in the number of people who visit an attraction, for example.

3. Focus groups: These give you the chance to gather more details about the customers' experiences. The groups are formed by usually no more than 10 people, and allow the interviewer to record more in-depth answers of the customers' reasons for choosing a product. The interviewer will use techniques to obtain the innermost thoughts of the interviewed.

Regarding secondary research sources, these can be internal or external to the organisation. Internal sources are sales records, customer databases, gate receipts, visitor records, and mailing lists. External sources are trade directories, local and central government departments, and annual reports.

- Research design: This tells us when the research will take place, by who, for how long, and for how much.
- Data collection: It indicates the number of people which will be surveyed, how they will be selected, etc.
- Data analysis and reporting: This involves analysing the findings and drawing conclusions in order to write the research report.

9.20 Questionnaire design

In order to design a questionnaire, experts advise following these steps:

- Make a list of the survey's objectives, e.g. what do you expect to know?
- Produce a first draft.
- Proceed with a pilot survey to see if the respondents understand the questions.
- After this, correct the first draft.
- Use the new version of the survey but do not stop making amendments if necessary.

General questionnaire advice:

- Personal questions about age, marital status, or occupation should go at the end.
- Make sure questions are clear and not ambiguous.
- Do not use jargon.
- Write only questions that help your findings; not unnecessary ones.
- Questions need to be simple and objective.
- Do not write leading questions, e.g. 'Would you agree that the service was appropriate?'
- Questions should not be difficult to answer, as it would be something like 'how many drinks did you have on your first week of holidays?'
- Language needs to be understandable by the respondent.

Holiday Feedback	
Name of the Holiday Resort	Customer's name (Optional)

Please let us know, what you think about the following services that are offered

Rating: A: Exceptional B: Satisfactory C: Average D: Unsatisfactory

Your reception upon arrival		The room and customer services	
Calendar of recreational activities provided by the management.		Hotel bookings (is it easy to get accommodation?)	
Accommodation		Cuisine Offered	
Waiting Services		Laundry Services.	
Serene and quiet location			

Please tell us what the highlights of your stay with us were.

Did your stay with us, meet your expectations? If not how can we improve?

What would you like to see on your next visit that you failed to see in this one?

Any other comments and suggestions	sampleforms.org

Example of Questionnaire

10. What affects travel and tourism?

10.10 Climatic conditions

Climatic conditions around the world have an impact on the choice of holiday destinations. You need to be aware of following situations:

- Hurricanes, typhoons, and cyclones: These are all tropical storms. Their intensity varies but they can reach up to 150 miles per hour. These kinds of storm can also come with torrential rain. Life is at risk in these climatic conditions as buildings become damaged, and people can be dragged away by the storm.

Aerial image of destroyed homes in Punta Gorda (USA), following hurricane Charley.

- Monsoons: are very strong winds accompanied by torrential rains, which can take place during the dry and wet seasons. When temperatures are very high during the dry season monsoons can occur causing floods. Monsoons are dangerous when the rain lasts for days.
- Humidity: This is water vapour in the air. When humidity is very high it can be uncomfortable.
- Sunshine: Travellers often seek sunny destinations but they need to know that too much sun can be dangerous.
- Snow: Snow can cause travel disruptions if it snows too much. Ski facilities and communications can be closed if snow becomes dangerous.
- Prevailing winds: are winds that blow predominantly from a single direction over the same place. They can bring warmth or cold air currents.

10.20 Seasonal variations

Some extreme weather conditions are seasonal, and they only take place during certain periods of the year. For this reason, it is good to know when it is the best time to travel. Travellers might need to avoid travelling to some places at certain times of the year. For example, hurricane and typhoon seasons are more likely to be between June and November in places such as the Caribbean and Florida. Monsoons are particularly likely to occur between June and September in India. One of the safest places to travel with the best conditions is the Mediterranean coast, where you find warm weather in spring and summer without being excessive. Tropical storms take place around the Tropic of Cancer in the northern hemisphere and in the Tropic of Capricorn in the southern hemisphere. Around the Equator are the hottest countries in the world, while the coldest are in the poles.

10.30 The effect of worldwide time
- Time zones: Time is set up against Greenwich Mean Time (GMT). This means that, for example, London time is GTM because the Greenwich meridian crosses the UK. Other times are referred to as GMT+1, GMT-1, etc. There are 24 time-zones in the world, and travellers need to adjust their time when arriving at a new time zone.
- Lines of longitude and the Prime Meridian: These are imaginary lines crossing the earth from north to south, and each one represents a time zone. Greenwich is the Prime Meridian at 0 degrees longitude. The opposite of the Prime Meridian is the International Date Line which is across the Pacific Ocean.
- Time differences between east and west: When you move towards the east each time zone you enter is one hour ahead of the UK. When you travel west each time zone is one hour behind. Some countries, like the USA or Russia, have multiple time zones.
- Daylight saving time: Most countries have daylight saving time when they change their time in order to adjust to daylight in spring and summer. In the UK, we put our clocks back at the end of October and forward at the end of March.
- Calculating worldwide time: You can use a time line to calculate the time in different parts of the world.

10.40 Human health
Travelling long distances can have an impact on your body, as it needs time to adjust to the new time zone. After losing or gaining hours your body needs to recover. Travellers might suffer from jetlag, and might feel dizzy and confused being awake in the night and sleepy in the day. The most dangerous health issue is deep vein thrombosis (DVT), which is a blood clot caused by sitting for too long.

10.50 Reasons for exit/entry requirements
In order to enter any country, you need a valid passport. Travellers should check the entry requirements of their country of destination as some might demand, for example, to have a valid passport for six months after the return date.

10.60 Visas
Some countries require a visa in order to both enter and exit the country. There are different types of visa according to the nature of trip.

10.70 Departure taxes
Some countries make you pay when you leave. Mexico and Australia, for example, impose a departure tax. This extra amount can be added to the flight ticket but it might not, and it can be an unplanned expense.

10.80 Airport Passenger Duty (APD)
APD is a tax charged to people flying outside the UK. APD is added to the flight ticket cost and the amount is different for every destination airport.

10.90 Travel health risks
In some regions, you can be infected with a fatal disease. Visit the following link to know areas of risk for each disease: https://wwwnc.cdc.gov/travel/diseases/

In order to prevent being infected with a disease, travellers may need to vaccinate before travelling. In some cases, clothing is important. For example, if travelling to a malaria risk country, travellers are advised to wear long sleeved clothes, long trousers, and hats to protect the skin. There are also tablets to protect against malaria. These tablets are available only with prescription. Equipment also exists for disinfecting water.

11. Responsible tourism

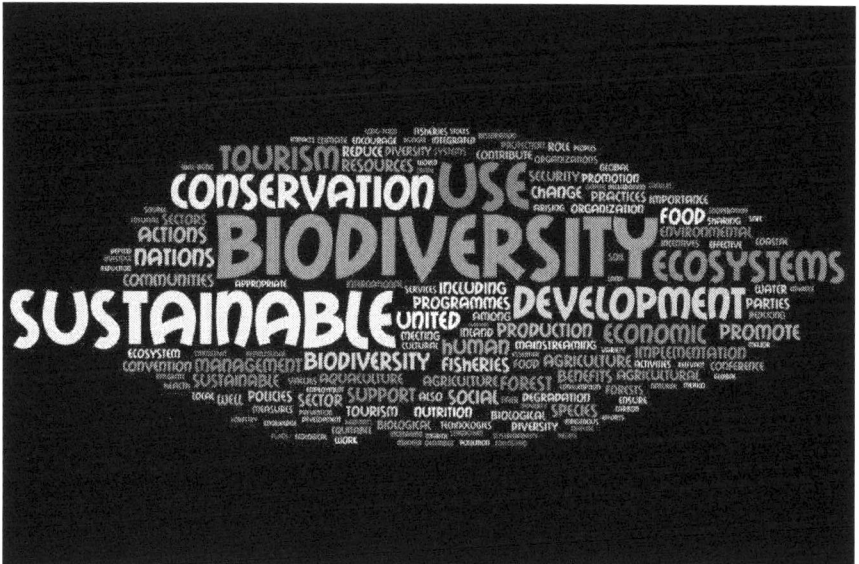

Responsible tourism is about developing tourism that is in harmony with the environment, the local people, their traditions and way of living, whilst also enhancing the visitors' experience. Responsible tourism is also called green tourism, sustainable tourism, eco-tourism, ethical tourism, soft tourism, or slow tourism. Responsible tourism takes the wellbeing of the host country very seriously. In this regard, responsible tourism wants to be a source of improvement adding to the economy and social wellbeing of the destination country. Tourism can provide jobs and improve the area but it can also destroy the environment and increase prices for the local people.

11.10 Positive economic impacts
The positive economic impact is one of the main reasons for the involvement of governments and organisations in tourism. Tourism creates a lot of new jobs as well as increasing domestic income and foreign currency earnings. It has a multiplier effect on the economy, and improves infrastructure.

- Increased domestic income and foreign currency earnings: Tourism generates benefits for all the parties involved in the industry, and at all levels. Thus, local councils and private companies benefit from the wealth generated by tourism. The money a country receives from tourism can make a difference to its balance of payments. Developing countries turn to tourism in order to increase their foreign currency earnings.
- Economic multiplier effect: This takes place at the local level when a town benefits from the revenue created by tourism. It means that it creates many jobs and increases people's wealth. Therefore, the economy is reinforced and boosted. This happens because the budget spent by a visitor multiplies; if they spend £150 in a hotel, the economic multiplier effect for the area is £150 x 1.5. The value of the multiplier varies according to the region; it is higher

for local business, as the owner of a guesthouse, for example, will use the money to buy food in shops of the area while a hotel of a chain might purchase its goods from outside the area.

- Increased employment: Creating jobs in tourism is relatively cheap and easy as the start-up costs are low. Direct employment in tourism takes place in hotels, restaurants, tour guides, travel agencies, tourist attractions, and tour operators. Tourism also creates indirect employment for example in construction, banking, design and transport.
- Improved infrastructure: Tourism is one of the factors that influences government decisions about creating or improving infrastructure. For example, an area might build and improve airports, roads, and public transport, and also power supply in order to attract visitors. This, then, benefits the locals. Countries have different sources of income and international help. For example, EU countries can apply for the European Regional Development Fund (ERDF), and developing countries can receive help from the World Bank and the UN.

11.20 Negative economic impacts

- Leakage: This happens when money is lost from a destination area. This might be because companies that own hotels, for example, operate in other countries and they take the benefits there. Sometimes it can also happen that local suppliers of goods do not sell because tourism organisations buy what they need in other areas.
- Decline of traditional employment and seasonal unemployment: The increase of the tourism sector in an area impacts on traditional employment activities belonging to the primary sector such as fishing or farming as workers change their jobs for service jobs in tourism. Thus, developing countries are at risk of losing their primary industries, as workers prefer the working conditions of the tourism sector. When many people are employed in tourism seasonal unemployment is more likely to happen as tourism has its peak seasons during the year but it cannot afford the same number of employees throughout the year.
- Increased living costs: The prices of basic goods and services can rise during peak holiday season. This affects local people who then need to pay more for their usual shopping. Locals might also need to pay taxes for tourism facilities. Areas with a high number of second houses which are only used for holidays increase the overall price of the housing market in that particular area, and locals might not be able to purchase a house or apartment. This is one of the reasons why people in some parts of Wales resent people from England having a 2nd home which is only used for a few weeks in a year.

11.30 Positive environmental impacts

The tourism sector is often criticised for destroying the environment but tourism can also help to raise awareness of environmental issues and instigate environmental improvements. For example, a visited area can stimulate activities to protect the environment, or organisations can fundraise by selling tickets to see protected wildlife areas. By showing tourists damaging situations, for instance, the loss of natural habitat or the threat of deforestation, you can also raise awareness of environmental issues. There are some pressure groups which raise awareness of these issues, such as Tourism Concern, Friends of the Earth, and Britain in Bloom.

11.40 Negative environmental impacts

Tourism can also have a dangerous and damaging impact on the environment. This holds true especially for vulnerable habitats such as sand dunes, coral reefs, rain forests and mountain areas. In

Britain, for example, coasts and the countryside suffer from a high number of visitors. The most threatening situations for the environment are:

- Congestion and overcrowding caused by too many people and cars.
- Water, air and noise pollution.
- Erosion of resources.
- Loss of habitats for flora and fauna, and the consequent extinguishment of the species.
- Litter.

These negative impacts affect all areas of a country: cities, coast, and countryside. National Parks are particularly vulnerable as they receive a high number of visits, such as the Peak District, South Downs and Lake District National Parks. In cities, these issues can be detrimental to historical places such as York, Bath, Oxford, or Cambridge, and capital cities London, Cardiff, Belfast and Edinburgh. In cities, pollution, litter and congestion are the most damaging problems.

11.50 Positive socio-cultural impacts

- Provision of community facilities and public services: facilities, which are built or provided for tourists, can benefit local people. For example, the implementation of public transport.
- Improved standards of living: the income from tourism can increase people's wealth in a particular area.
- Preservation of customs and crafts: tourists might buy local handicraft, and this means an extra income for locals and communities.
- Revival of festivals and ceremonies: tourists might like to see all the customs and traditions of an area. These might include traditional festivals, e.g. music and dance, theatre, etc.
- Cultural education: tourists see and learn from different cultures.

11.60 Negative socio-cultural impacts

- Crime: Mass tourism can be a trigger for criminal activities such as pickpockets and prostitution.
- Sex tourism: tourists can also become criminals themselves and exploit girls and women for sexual benefits in the country of destination.
- Conflict with the host community: if tourism is not well managed it can give place to hostilities between visitors and the locals, and cause an anti-social behaviour. Excessive noise, congestion, or cultural clash can be some of the problems. In some cases, locals can imitate the dress and customs of visitors; this is called the "demonstration effect", and it can cause problems among the locals.
- Displacement: some locals might be forced to move in order to leave the area clear for tourism purposes. This is extremely unfair, and can happen in developing countries.
- Loss of cultural identity: mass tourism can dissolve the traditional way of living of an area. For example, religious codes or languages might be undermined if tourists do not respect them.
- Staged authenticity: Some activities performed for tourists such as dance and music, or any kind of folklore, can lack authenticity and thus demean cultural traditions.

11.70 Roles of agents in tourism development

Agents of tourism development are the organisations or individuals that promote and fund tourism at international, national, regional and local levels. The main roles of agents are providing travel and tourism products, services and resources, funding tourism development, marketing destinations, and helping the conservation and protection of the environment. There are three main kinds of agents:

- Private sector agents: These are private companies or individuals that invest in tourist facilities expecting a good return. Their primary aim is profit, and they are the most common types of agents in tourism. Among private sector agents there are:
    1. Landowners: From land substantial benefit is made. Landowners provide land for building facilities, such as hotels and attractions, which in turn can generate a high amount of money.
    2. Property developers: They take the risk of investing in, and developing, infrastructures where they think there will be a demand for them. They might invest in the development of a new hotel, for example.

Property developers take risks when investing in local infrastructure.

    3. Tour operators: If tour operators include destinations and events in the programmes that they advertise, they will increase their chance of success.
    4. Hotel chains: They can develop projects for new hotels in areas where they see potential.
    5. Airlines: Starting new routes to destination airports is the way in which airlines develop tourism in new areas.
    6. Entertainment companies: They develop and improve tourism by developing new attractions such as clubs, bars, restaurants, casinos, etc.

- Public sector agents: The public sector does not focus on making profit but on having a positive impact on society, community and the economy. The public sector also sets the tourism policies in order to create an appropriate business climate for private businesses. Some examples of public sector agents are: United Nations World Tourism Organisation (UNWTO); national tourist organisation (VisitBritain); regional tourists board (Heart of English Tourist Board); and local authority tourism department (Worcester City Council).
    1. National governments: Countries with a big tourism industry have a government department dedicated exclusively to tourism. Its functions are establishing tourism policies (what kind of tourism to encourage, how to control impacts, etc.). It will also be responsible for the marketing and promotion of tourism, providing funds for the creation of infrastructures, running some facilities such as museums, theatres or galleries, coordinating tourist information, dealing with regulations for

visas, health and safety, licenses, etc., and, finally, financing the development of tourism, and providing business advisory services and training.

2. Local authorities: They finance as many tourism facilities as possible according to the limited budget they often have. This includes funding marketing such as leaflets, brochures and websites, and also the facilities themselves, e.g. theatres, museums, or also accommodation booking services, leisure centres, etc.

3. National and regional tourist boards: The UK has four National Tourist Boards, which are VisitBritain, Visit Wales, Visit Scotland and the Northern Ireland Tourist Board. Their funding comes from the central government channelled through the Department for Digital Culture Media and Sport, the Welsh Assembly Government, the Scottish Executive and Northern Ireland Assembly. Regional tourist boards work with Regional Development agencies (RDAs) in England to develop tourism. There are nine Regional Tourist Boards in England, four Regional Tourism Partnerships (RTPs) in Wales, 14 RTBs in Scotland and five Regional Tourism Organisations in Northern Ireland.

4. Conservation organisations: These often deal with tourism development such as protecting National Parks, museums and historic houses. For example, English Heritage is a publicly funded organisation dedicated to the conservation of sites.

- Voluntary sector agents: The voluntary sector includes community groups, charities, trusts and non-governmental organisations involved in environmental issues and helping communities, promoting sustainable tourism, etc. Voluntary organisations vary in size, and they can be formed by a small number of people or can be a big organisation such as the Youth Hostels Association (YHA). These kinds of organisations receive grants and help from the private and public sectors.

11.80 Objectives of tourism development

While creating jobs and revenue are two very important objectives of the tourism sector, there are also socio-cultural, political and environmental objectives. You also need to know that tourism development can be a complex and polemic process as all the parts involved prioritise their own interests. Thus, for example, developers want projects to finish as soon as possible in order to receive their gains, while community groups will be concerned and evaluate a project's impact on the environment.

- Political objectives: Politics is often involved in tourism, and central and local governments discuss if tourism should be encouraged or dismissed. They also take decisions regarding the kind of tourism and facilities they may provide. Governments can control the revenue from tourism and invest it in other areas such education and health. In developing countries, tourism is used to mask poverty. Tourism can also enhance the image of a country or area. Thus, tourism creates a positive image of the country in order to attract visitors. Tourism marketing can also change or strengthen the identity of a destination. This relates to the image projected to the exterior. For example, some industrial areas, such as Milan in Italy, can focus their marketing on fashion, culture and heritage and become a popular destination.

- Economic objectives: Tourism can create employment, attract income and have a multiplier effect, increase foreign currency earnings, and contribute to economic regeneration.

1. Employment creation: This is one of the most important economic objectives of tourism development. The tourism industry employs over 235 million people around the world. In the UK tourism employs around 2.6 million people. This is why tourism appeals to many developing countries although tourism jobs can be seasonal and poorly paid.

2. Revenue generation: Tourism is an extra source of income for a country. Hotel, airport and border taxes are very common in the whole world, and this is a way in which countries gain revenue. The gains from tourism can then be invested for regional development. Tourism can generate foreign currency earnings in the form of taxes and direct payments to tourist businesses. Revenue from tourism contributes to a country's balance of payments (money going in and out of a country). Tourism is one of the invisible items on a country's balance of payments account, together with banking and insurance, in contrast to visible items which are manufactured goods, raw materials, etc.

3. Economic regeneration: Some areas develop tourism in order to reactivate the economy. For example, old industry areas that no longer make a profit might switch to tourism. We can see examples with the National Mining Museum in England and similar examples in the other UK countries. There is also a slate museum in Llanberis in Wales which attracts many visitors.

- Environmental objectives: Tourism also has objectives concerning the improvement and protection of the environment.

1. Habitat and heritage preservation: In some areas with vulnerable habitats tourism raises environmental awareness that can lead to the preservation of habitats at risk. Species at risk are also preserved, especially in Africa, and they have become valuable tourism assets as without wildlife there would be no tourism. Kenya in East Africa has many wildlife parks which attract many visitors. Even in England, Bewdley in the West Midlands attracts visitors with its collection of some rare animals.

2. Environmental education: tourism can teach visitors about the environment. Tours, for example, can include information on environmental issues.

3. Environmental regeneration: Visitors can trigger improvement, for example, having clean beaches, creating walking and cycling routes, etc.

- Socio-cultural objectives: Tourism needs to work in harmony with local people in order to be truly sustainable. Traditional ways of living need to be respected and maintained.

11.90 Strategies to maximise tourism's positive impacts
This can be achieved mainly in the following ways:

- Retention of visitor spending: Money spent by visitors recirculates in the local or/and regional area. This is the multiplier effect which we have already seen. Tourism development plans should make sure that there are as few leakages as possible. Tourism plans might thus look at ways of using local suppliers and involving communities in making decisions regarding tourism. Famous chefs such as Rick Stein in Cornwall has a restaurant which aims to provide not just good food but also information about which items are sustainable and which foods are not.

- Widening access to facilities: Providing as many facilities as possible to tourists also means that local people will have access to them. For example, providing museum discounts for disadvantaged people.
- Community projects: Although the economy is one of the most important motives for tourism, some governments can decide to strengthen tourism in order to improve the life of the community. There can be public investments in leisure centres, infrastructure and parks. All of these are quite social but might not be justifiable in economic terms. Income from tourism can be used to maintain some of the areas and facilities visited.
- Employment and the training of local people: One of the most positive effects of tourism is the training and subsequent employment of local people for tourist jobs. Education and training of local people is a very good way to retain tourism revenue and also to provide excellent service.
- Education: This refers both to visitors and tourism businesses. It is good if visitors learn about the country and area of destination before going, especially if they travel to developing countries as they will be able to engage in responsible tourism. Businesses can also learn how to act responsibly in order to benefit the community.

Education is key to promoting sustainable tourism.

11.100 Strategies to minimise tourism's negative impacts

Techniques to minimise tourism's negative impact include:

- Visitor and traffic management: Trying to diminish the number of cars in an area, especially a city, is very important for responsible tourism that respects the environment. Using public transport is encouraged in urban and rural areas. For example, the Peak District National Park works to dissuade visitors of coming with their own car. Some roads in National Parks are closed in peak hours in order to encourage walking and cycling around other paths. There are, for example, park-and-ride schemes in order to avoid cars in cities and towns.
- Planning controls: Tourism planners need to make sure all tourism facilities are also available to the local people, and they also need to respect the environment. Planners need to measure the impact of a tourism plan on the landscape. Planners need to evaluate the impact of hotels and holiday complexes, the signposting of tourism facilities, the change of buildings and land for tourism purposes, tourism attractions, car parking for visitors, etc.
- Environmental impact assessments (EIA): This is a technique used to evaluate the environmental costs and benefits of a development. EIAs are required before starting with the building of a facility. EIAs can look at many different things that impact on the environment, such as the fuel used in airplanes or the detergents for cleaning used in hotels.

- Sustainable tourism policies: The definition of sustainable tourism by the World Tourism Organisation (WTO) is 'tourism that meets the needs of present tourists and host regions while protecting and enhancing opportunity for the future'. Bodies such as the Environment Task Force have implemented and developed policies to practice sustainable tourism. Some of the principles of these policies are:
    1. The environment has its own value and this is more important than the value of tourism. Its long survival cannot be exchanged for short-term benefits.
    2. Tourism should be seen as an activity that improves the community, the place and the visitor.
    3. Tourism cannot damage natural resources.
    4. Tourism activities and facilities should respect the place: its scale and character.
    5. There needs to be harmony between the community, the place and the visitor.
    6. Changes need to respect the principles stated above.

12. Travel and tourism employment opportunities I

12.10 Job roles within the tourism industry

Travel agents such as The Co-operative travel employ travel consultants and advisors. (The Co-operative Travel on Colehill, Tamworth)

- Travel agents: High street travel agents such as Co-op Travel and Thomas Cook employ travel consultants (or advisors), foreign exchange advisors and a management team usually comprised of a store manager, an assistant manager and an overall area manager. The store manager is responsible for the whole store and staff. There will also be trainees and apprentices called junior consultants. An average agency employs around 5-10 employees. There can also be administrative roles such as human resources and accountants.

  Travel agents sell a range of different products, which can be holiday packages, accommodation, transport and all kind of ancillary services such as travel insurance, attraction tickets, care renting, etc. By selling ancillary services, an agency provides everything a customer might need, and the agency becomes more competitive.

- Tour operators: Tour operators, such as First Choice and Thomson, sell tours and package holidays to travel agents or directly to the public by telephone and the internet. Working for a tour operator opens many job opportunities, and many people are employed to design package holidays. They need buyers to source the product that will make a package. This involves booking flights or train tickets, organising transfers from the airport, and booking accommodation, or making a list of possible accommodation options. A tour operator also needs quality controllers, operation managers, marketing-staff (web designers, editors, writers, and photographers). Customer services are also necessary to answer calls and emails from customers and deal with queries and complaints. There might be also a training department to train staff when required.

- Airlines and airports: The staff working for an airline is divided into ground crew (landside) and air crew (airside). Aircrew include the pilot, co-pilot, flight engineer and navigator, and all the flight assistants. There are usually about six cabin crew on a standard flight.

The staff working for an airline is divided into ground crew (landside) and air crew (airside).

The ground crew in the airport include check-in agents, customer service agents, information assistants, baggage handlers, and dispatch and airport management. Small companies might have ground handlers to be responsible for the ground side of their operation. This is because small companies usually do not have a base of operations in one airport. Other employers at the airport employ cleaners and security staff.

- Accommodation providers: There are some accommodation providers, such as Keycamps. Accommodation providers offer a variety of different types of accommodation from caravans to 5-star hotels. There is serviced and non-serviced accommodation. Serviced accommodation offers food and drinks, and leisure and business facilities. This increases the number of jobs as people are needed in reception, conference, banqueting, events management and housekeeping.

- Visitor attractions: Attractions vary from theme parks to museums and theatres. These provide job positions. There are general careers such as customer service, ticket office personnel, and security and management posts. There are also roles such as tour guiding. Tour guides need to be very good at customer service and they need to be knowledgeable about the attraction they are showing.

  Museums, for example, also have curators, restorers and conservation workers for the collections. Some attractions have gift shops and tearooms and restaurants in the UK. These employ retail and catering staff. Engineering staff are required in theme parks. Some attractions also have an educational officer as schools visit, for example, the Globe Theatre in south London which is built on the site which William Shakespeare would have known.

- Passenger transport operators: The main forms of transport are airlines, trains, coaches, ferries, and cruise ships. These are widely used for tourists. Train operators employ customer service staff, and ticketing staff to work on the platform and in the train. Coach companies employ coach drivers, managerial roles, and customer service staff. Depending on the company's size, managerial roles might take on customer service. Coach operators that are not only hire for occasions but have a regular schedule, such as National Express, employ dispatchers at some coach stations. Ferries and cruise ships employ staff for sailing and attending the people on board. There are also deck officers, engineers, maintenance staff, entertainers, retail staff, waiters and chefs.

- Tourism development: VisitBritain promotes the UK in other countries to attract visitors. VB employs marketing and brand staff, web designers, finance staff, IT staff, press and PR, market intelligence, digital and new media, quality standards, online shops, human resources and research and evaluation.

12.20 Working patterns in travel and tourism

The working patterns in the tourism industry vary depending on the job, the work carried out, and the schedule of the organisation.

- Full-time/part-time: Many organisations offer both full- and part-time jobs. For example, a travel agency might have full-time staff from 9am to 5pm but if it decides to increase its opening times it might hire part-time staff to work in the evening or weekends.
- Seasonal: Seasonal staff is very common as the tourist industry has peak seasons such as in summer and winter holidays. Seasonal or temporary staff might be hired only in peak seasons to support permanent staff.
- Shift work: If an organisation has a long schedule (more than 8 hours a day), staff might work shifts. In places such as airports, where there are flights almost at all times, shifts also occur, e.g. night and day shifts. In this way, customers are always tended to.

12.30 Job specifications for employment in the tourism sector

- Duties and responsibilities: The organisation writes a job and person specification in order to find an appropriate candidate for the position. These statements describe the nature of the job, the activities that need to be done, in short, duties and responsibilities. The job specification will also include the job title, department, salary, bonuses earned, and hours. It may also give ideas of career development.
- Key terms of employment: In the tourist sector contracts will vary depending on the service provided. For example, cabin crew can work long shifts on international flights, and then have two or three days off. Office staff might have a regular 9am-5pm work. Holiday entitlement varies between full-time and seasonal staff, for example.
- Pay and employment benefits: Salaries vary as well from very well-paid pilots to lowly paid junior travel agents, or catering staff. The competitive nature of the industry meant that the industry often tries to reduce salaries in order to be able to offer cheaper holidays to customers. Some jobs, however, may compensate for lower salaries by providing commission based on sales performances on top of the initial salary.

12.40 Person specifications for jobs in the travel and tourism sector

- Qualifications: The organisation seeking new staff will write a person specification which indicates the skills they are looking for. A person specification states the essential and desirable attributes including qualifications. Specific to the tourism sector are the BTEC or Diploma in travel and tourism. Employers might also look for academic qualifications such as GCSEs, A-levels and university degrees.
- Vocational skills:

1. Information technology: It is a very good skill to have and almost unavoidable as everything is becoming more and more technological. The Internet and booking systems are, for example, key to almost every job in the sector. Data systems are also very important for travel agents, receptionists and airport staff.
2. Literacy and numeracy: Qualifications in Maths and English are very important to increase your employability in tourism. For some organisations, this is a minimum requirement and you might need to complete a literacy and numeracy test as part of the recruitment process.
3. Leadership: Initiative is a very important quality for any job position in the tourism sector. Many tourism employees have a face-to-face relationship with the customers, and this means employees will need to take on responsibilities and initiative resolving problems.
4. Communication, listening and problem-solving: These are very important skills as tourism employees have direct and constant contact with customers. Employees need to listen to customers' requirements or complaints as well as providing them indications, or explaining any issues that may arise.
5. Project planning and organisational skills: All the skills and tasks involved in project planning are required in the tourism sector. Organisation, planning, problem-solving, marketing, team work and customer service skills are needed. These skills can be put into practice in many different roles; they are transferable skills that you can use, for example, working in a resort, as part of the cabin crew or in hotel reception.
6. Customer service: Without customers, there would be no business. It is very important to provide an excellent customer service. When customers book or buy services, they are actually paying the wages of the employees. Usually it is the quality of customer service what makes the difference between companies, and increases the chance of success of a company or organisation. Some companies such as First Choice and Thomas Cook have in-house trainers that provide customer service training to their employees.

- Personal skills:
  1. Teamwork: Teamwork is common in many roles because groups of people are likely to achieve more than an individual. Teamwork, however, is not always easy, as people can disagree with particular ways of doing things. Teamwork is a learned skill that involves respect and acceptance.
  2. Reliability: This is an important characteristic especially in teamwork. For things to work out, you need to compromise and be where you are supposed to be and do what you are expected to do. If someone is not reliable, the service can become delayed and it will not create a good impression on customers.
  3. Personal presentation: a customers' first impression is very important. Therefore, organisations often require their staff to dress and behave in a professional manner. Staff are usually dressed in the organisation's uniform, which gives a cohesive image of the company and guarantees that employees meet the required dress code standards.
  4. Commitment: Commitment to your work is very important. You should always perform the best you can, even if you are tired or on a night shift. Customers will feel the difference.

5. Flexibility: Being flexible is necessary as you might need to attend a customer for longer that you thought, or deal with an unfamiliar department in order to help a customer. You might need to stay longer on your shift if you are in the middle of a task.
6. Motivation: Employees' motivation is very important, as this helps them to perform better and feel happier in their jobs. Some ways of motivating the employees are providing commission on sales, flexible working hours, incentives and perks, discounted accommodation, etc.
7. Attitude: As the tourism sector is primarily customer focused, attitude is very important when it comes to recruiting employees. Organisations look for positive, active and cheerful people.

- Transferable skills:
  1. Part-time work: Skills developed in part-time jobs, if they are customer oriented, can be very useful for the tourism industry, or a wide variety of other sectors. Dealing with complaints, finding the right products for each customer, adapting to each customer, working night shifts are all transferable skills that increase your employability.
  2. Voluntary work: You can also undertake voluntary work as a means of improving your skills and making yourself more employable.

12.50 Binding rights and responsibilities
- Statutory rights:
  1. Health and safety: Risks to the health and safety of employees need to be controlled.

This is the function of the Health and Safety at Work Act 2011 as well as earlier legislation such as the Health and Safety at Work Act 1974. These statutory rights must be provided by the employer. Workers are also responsible for their own safety and those working with them. Workers need to be protected from anything that can harm them. Employers need to inform their staff about risks as well as prevention.

  2. Equality: The Equality Act 2010 is a law which bans unfair treatment and protects equal opportunities regardless of sex, gender, age, or race. The act covers nine characteristics (age, disability, gender reassignment, marriage and civil partnership, pregnancy, maternity and paternity, race, religion or belief, sex, sexual orientation). On this basis discrimination is illegal. The act prohibits unfair treatment at work, when providing goods, when exercising public functions, in the disposal of premises, in education and by associations.
  3. Employment protection: Employees are protected by the Employment Rights Act 1996. This law ensures employees are not unfairly treated by the employer.
  4. Pay and holidays: Full time employees are entitled to a minimum of 5.6 weeks of paid holidays. On top of that there are Bank holidays. Enlarging the days of holidays can be

a reward for the employee or, in the case of part-time staff, it can be a means of guaranteeing their loyalty.

5. Working hours and conditions: Employees might not work more than 48 hours a week. Working hours are set up in the work contract.

6. Maternity/paternity rights: Statutory maternity pay is paid by the employer if you are on maternity leave. In order to be able to receive statutory maternity leave you need to have worked for a period of time for the same employer. The payment for maternity leave can change after the six first weeks of leave but it continues until up to 39 weeks. Statutory paternity pay is made to the father for up to 2 weeks.

- Contractual rights:
  1. Of the employer: The employers give the employee a job description with detailed information on the job, expectations of the employee and contractual obligations such as notice period, or holidays. The employer also has contractual obligations.
  2. Of the employee: The employee needs to agree to the working conditions stated in the job contract and sign it in order to start his or her job.

12.60 Recruitment and selection in the travel and tourism sector

Production of documentation:

1. Job description: Organisations produce job descriptions when they need to hire new staff. A job description states the requirements of the position advertised and the tasks the new employee will need to carry out.

2. Person specification: This describes the required and desired person in terms of skills and attitude. Experience and qualifications are also particularly important for jobs which are not at the lowest end of the employment hierarchy.

A great deal of effort goes into selecting the right candidate.

- Advertising: Organisations advertise their open positions in different ways. Big companies might advertise jobs on their own website, others will do it through a recruitment search engine or agency.

- Application process: When applying for a job you might need either to send a CV or fill in an online form. After the deadline for sending applications the organisation will shortlist candidates for an interview. In the interview, you could be interviewed by a panel or one single person. Online and phone interviews are also possible. Interviews can also consist of a series of activities that you need to carry out. This allows the recruiters to evaluate how you handle yourself in different situations. You might also need to complete a numerical and literacy test. In order to know the candidate's personality, the organisation might require you to undertake a psychometric test. This consists in multiple-choice questionnaire where there is no correct answer but the answers give an idea of the candidate's personality. The successful candidate will receive a job offer after which reference letters are usually required.

12.70 New employment

- Job requirements: At the beginning of a new employment, new employees undertake an induction process in which they become familiar with the organisation. An induction includes health and safety, introduction to the workplace, lines of responsibility, the job role and the location of facilities. Training is an important part of an organisation, and new staff are required to undertake some weeks of training. External training is also provided. After training, new employees will have a probationary period often lasting from 6 to 12 months. The probationary period starts with a description of targets that need to be achieved by the end of the period. During the probationary period employees will be assessed.

12.80 Career progression

Many travel organisations offer their employees the possibility of further training in order to achieve better positions within the industry. Some training might lead to full qualifications such as National Vocational Qualifications. Other more specific jobs, such as being a pilot, need a JAA-PPL (Joint Aviation Authority-Private Pilot License). An air traffic controller needs NATS (National Air Transportation System) training. Performance of the employees is monitored by targets achieved. Staff who meet their targets can be promoted or awarded in some way. In travel organisations, which own different companies, employees have more opportunities to develop and be promoted.

13. Travel and tourism employment opportunities II

13.10 Job opportunities in the travel and tourism sector

This section looks in more detail to specific jobs in the tourism industry ranging from travel agencies to airlines. This section focuses on main job roles and the necessary qualifications and personal requirements.

Learning new skills can help to secure a job in the tourism sector

- Opportunities in retail travel: Travel agencies are a very common place to start a career in tourism. Employers focus on the following qualities:
    1. Good communication skills.
    2. A friendly and helpful personality.
    3. A good standard of English, maths and geography.
    4. Experience of travelling.
    5. A smart appearance.
    6. Good organisation skills.
    7. IT skills.
    8. The ability to work under pressure.
    9. A confident telephone manner.

If you learn fast and perform well you can expect to be promoted to positions such as supervisor, assistant manager or branch manager. Companies with many stores can also relocate staff.

- Opportunities in tour operations: Tour operations make holiday packages which are sold in travel agents. Tour operations can be big companies, such as Thomas Cook, or small and highly specialised. Most jobs are in the UK but big companies might have job openings in overseas resorts. Opportunities are usually in:
    1. Sales.
    2. Product development.
    3. Marketing.
    4. Customer service.
    5. Operations.
    6. Contracting.
    7. Overseas.
    8. Human resources and training.
    9. Finance, administration and IT systems.

Depending on the job, employers will focus on different skills; however, there are some general skills that you will always need such as good telephone manner, outgoing personality, diplomacy, good decision-making skills, administrative and computer skills. If the job involves working with children you need a DBS (Disclosure Barring Service) check prior to the appointment.

- Opportunities in transport: Transport covers air, land and sea. Jobs are offered by a range of companies such as airlines and airports, ferry companies, car hire firms, coach operators, train companies, cruise lines and inland waterways. For transport jobs, it is very important to have technical abilities and awareness of health and safety regulations. If the position involves direct contact with the general public, the customer care skills and good manners are also very important. There are professional transport organisations such as the Chartered Institute of Logistics and Transport (CILT) and the Institute of Transport Administration (IOTA) which offer specialist transport courses.
- Cruising is a very fast-growing industry, and it offers a variety of job positions (customer service, catering, sports coaching, entertainment, retail, child care and sales/marketing). The best way to start in cruises is often with a waiter or waitress position. One of the most important cruise lines is Cunard, and its hiring requirements are the following:
  1. Minimum age 20 years.
  2. Diploma or equivalent.
  3. At least one year experience in a good quality hotel or restaurant.
  4. Good command of written and spoken English.
  5. Pleasant, positive and outgoing personality with a desire to succeed.

The increase in air travel has produced a large number of employment opportunities with airlines and in airports. Airlines recruit pilots, cabin crew and customer service staff. In the airports, there are specialist companies that provide staff for baggage handling, in-flight catering and maintenance.

- Opportunities in the accommodation industry: This includes any establishment used to spend at least one night. Hotels, guesthouses, self-catering cottages and inns are some examples. Hospitality, when combined with catering, is the biggest sector in the tourism industry, and there are many job offers. There are management and supervisory positions in hotels, or administrative and marketing jobs in letting agencies. Sought after skills are:
  1. Good communication skills.
  2. A friendly and helpful personality.
  3. A smart appearance.
  4. Good organisational skills.
  5. IT skills.
  6. A confident telephone manner.

If you want to increase your employability you often need to be willing to work unsociable hours. Initiative and enthusiasm are very important characteristics for promotion.

- Opportunities at visitor attractions: Attractions exist throughout the country. They can be historic buildings, theme parks, cultural attractions, entertainment, sports and recreation centres, etc. To work at such places, you need to enjoy working with people, be flexible and be a very good communicator. Technical skills and safety awareness are also important. Knowledge of foreign languages are also a plus as many foreigners come to visit who do not always have a very good command of English.

13.20 Career progression

Career progression is very common and achievable in the tourism industry. Young employees are often given positions of responsibility if they perform well. There are four main ways in which career progression occurs:

1. A promotion within the same type of job in the same organisation, e.g. from sales consultant to senior sales consultant.
2. Different jobs within the same organisation.
3. Similar job with another company.
4. Different job in different company.

It is also very important to continue training during your career, not only when you start. Extra qualifications will enhance your professional opportunities.

- Training: You usually undertake training to develop specific skills, for example, IT skills. Training can be part of your job, off-job or a combination of both. A training programme means that you will continue working while taking additional time to develop a set of skills. Some training takes place away from work; it is called off-the-job-training. Some employers might prefer this kind of training as it can be more objective. Distance learning is another possibility. Employees can enrol online and undertake the course from home. Apprenticeship is the name for a training route that is now very popular. Apprenticeships offer positions at entry and other levels. Apprenticeships are available in retail travel, tourist attractions, cabin crew, and hospitality and airline operations.
- Further education: Undertaking a qualification in tourism is usually the first step to start focusing on a career in tourism. There are different kinds of qualifications (BTEC, AS/A2, OCR). After finishing your BTEC course, you might choose between the following paths:
    1. Take a job in tourism and continue with training.
    2. Go into a higher education (HE) course which can be more than 3 years long.
- Higher education opportunities in travel and tourism: There are many HE courses in travel and tourism. You can find courses on tourism management, adventure tourism, heritage tourism and international tourism. Each course has different entry requirements, which you need to read carefully.

13.30 Factors to consider

Before you decide to take a career in tourism, you need to consider the following factors:

- Seasonality: Many jobs in the tourism industry are not permanent but temporary. Employers need extra staff during peak seasons, some tourist attractions and resorts, such as ski resorts, open only in winter. However, you might find two jobs within 12 months and avoid being unemployed.
- Type of job: Jobs can be full-time, permanent, temporary, voluntary or short-term contract.
- Working hours: You might need to work unsociable hours when people usually enjoy their leisure time (evenings, nights, holidays, and weekends). You might also have shift work.

Sometimes you may have to work unsocial hours.

- Pay levels: Tourism is not a highly paid industry with the exception of some jobs. Tourist boards and local authority tourism department are better paid and present better conditions of employment.
- Job perks: There are benefits of working in the tourism industry, for example, you might get discounts for flight tickets or hotels.

13.40 Stages of recruitment and selection
- Organisational procedures: When an organisation needs a new staff member, there is a recruitment process that consists of eight stages:
    1. Identifying company needs: When a vacancy comes up it is a good moment for the organisation to see what kind of staff it needs. A free post can appear because a member of staff leaves or a new post needs to be filled. If the position is for an already existent job, you can merely look through previous records and find the original job advertisement. You can also obtained information in the post by asking the current post holder.
    2. Job descriptions: A job description describes what the job involves, the tasks to be carried out and the areas of responsibility. A job description needs to show the title of the post (grade, post number, department/section, location), the summary of the job, responsibilities (position in the organisation, to whom responsible), detailed duties, conditions of employment (salary, holiday entitlement, hours of work, pension arrangements, welfare facilities) and the date of production (responsibilities can change over time).
    3. Person specification: Together with a job description it is common to have a job specification stating the essential and desirable skills of the candidate. The person specification also includes character, previous experience and qualifications. Some person specifications state how a candidate will be assessed (interview, test, etc.).
    4. Recruitment advertising: After producing a job and person specification, the company can focus on internal or external recruitment. The recruitment process can take place and be organised within the same company or through a recruitment agency. There are different ways in which tourism jobs can be advertised. These are advertisements in regional and national newspapers, trade journals and magazines, employment agencies specialising in tourism, employment road shows in public areas, the internet and radio, job centres, links with colleges and universities, newsletters circulated by professional bodies such as the Tourism Society, ITT (Institute of Travel and Tourism), HCIMA (Hotel and Catering International Management Association).
    5. Shortlisting: Many organisations ask for a CV and covering letter from the applicant. The public and voluntary sectors, however, prefer a completed application form. In these cases, if the applicant sends a CV instead of an application form, the application may be automatically rejected. For an organisation, the first step in the actual selection process consists in matching CVs with the person specification. This includes qualifications, experience and skills. Afterwards, there is a shortlist of candidates that will be interviewed. The interview can be one-to-one, in front of a panel or by phone or over Skype.
    6. Interviews and testing: The interview is the main element in a selection process. The interview allows employers to meet the candidates and ask questions about their

careers and lives as well as future aspirations in more detail. Likewise, the candidate will have the chance to ask questions and meet potential colleagues. Interviewing is criticised by some people who think interviews are open to personal prejudices, personal tastes and lacks objectivity. To avoid this, interviews need to be planned and usually present the same questions for all candidates. The golden rules for interviews are planning the interview, taking notes from the candidate's answers, inviting the candidates to take notes, asking the candidate to add or explain the information already submitted, paying attention to the candidate's strengths and weakness, asking open questions, asking for career plans and avoiding personal questions.

7. Psychometric testing: Sometimes undertaking a test is part of the selection process. Keyboard skills, numeracy and geographical skills can be tested. A psychometric test can assess a candidate for a specific role and set of skills.

8. Offer of employment: Once the right person has been chosen, the employer writes an offer of employment. This can be subject to references and medical examination. The candidate will need to formally reply to the job offer.

9. Contracts of employment: This is a written statement which sets up the terms of conditions in which a new staff member is expected to work. The statement must include the names of the employee and employer, job title, starting date of employment, salary, hours of work, holiday entitlement, entitlement to sick leave and pay, pensions entitlement, entitlement of the employer and the employee to notice of termination of employment, the date of termination of employment for temporary contracts, place of work, existence of agreements that affect the employee's terms and conditions negotiated by a trade union.

10. Induction: Induction programmes aim to help new staff members to know the company better, to settle into a new job and to meet work colleagues. An induction includes information on the importance of the tourism sector, the main features of the job, conditions of employment, introduction to work colleagues, rules on dress, appearance, eating, drinking and smoking, health, safety and security procedures, staff representation, social and welfare facilities, and training opportunities.

13.50 Preparing an application for employment

- Personal skills audit: In order to prepare yourself well and be aware of what you can offer and what you can aspire to, you need to complete a personal skills audit thinking about how you match the following points:
  1. Communication.
  2. IT skills.
  3. Numeracy.
  4. Working on your own.
  5. Team work.
  6. Problem solving.
  7. Interview skills.

Regarding personal characteristics, you need to show an attitude to work, good personal presentations, assertiveness, show your personality, be careful with your body language, and manage time.

- Applying for work: To start with, you need to know where to look for jobs, how to write a CV and cover letter and complete forms.
    1. Research: You can look for jobs on the Internet, newspapers, trade journals and magazines. You can also send your CV and cover letter to organisations without job openings and ask them to contact you when a job position is available. You can search in employment agencies and on the websites of Professional Bodies.
    2. CVs: CV stands for Curriculum Vitae, which loosely translates from Latin as 'course of life'. A CV is a structured and written statement of your skills and career history that you write in order to be selected for an interview. You need to update your CV as your career/skills develop, and you also need to write a CV with a job offer in mind in order to highlight the qualities the employer is looking for. The following information must also be in your CV: full name, postal address, phone number and e-mail, education history, academic and vocational qualifications, employment history, skills and achievements. At the beginning of your CV you can include a short paragraph describing yourself.
    3. Application forms: You might be asked to fill in an online form instead of sending in your CV. Application forms are divided into sections including details of the applicant, name and reference of the position you are applying for, details of education and qualification, employment history, reasons for applying for the current job, interests, and contact details of referees.
    4. Letters of application: A cover letter needs to support and complement either your CV or application form. The letter needs to explain the reasons for which you are applying for the job, what you can contribute to the organisation, your relevant skills and achievements and the capabilities you have developed. The cover letter needs to include words such as achieved, introduced, planned, finished, set up, completed, created and reorganised. The letter needs to be faultless when it comes to grammar and syntax.
- Interview skills: Interviews are very common in the recruitment process. The employer can assess if a candidate is well suited to the job. The candidate can sell himself better and ask questions to the employer. The employer will also have a better idea of the organisation. Some employers will undertake a short interview over the phone to shorten the list of candidates to be interviewed on-site.
    1. Advance preparation: To prepare well for the interview you need to confirm the date of interview soon, carefully plan your journey leaving extra time in case a problem arises, dress appropriately, learn as much as possible about the organisation, read the job details again and match your profile, try to anticipate questions and answers, make a list of questions to ask.
    2. Attending interviews: You need to project a positive attitude during the interview. When you enter the room shake hands with the interviewer(s) if possible. Try to stay calm. You might need to complete a numeric, IT or psychometric test. For certain jobs, such as airline jobs and overseas jobs with tour operators, you might need to complete group tasks in order to see your negotiating and leadership skills. If you need to give a presentation, speak clearly and slowly, and use prompt cards rather than notes. Using PowerPoint can look very professional and help your presentation.

3. Personal presentation and body language: Your dress and appearance are very important in making a first impression to your potential employer. Men should wear suits and women shout wear a suit or skirt suit. Smile when appropriate but also show a serious appearance.
4. Projecting a positive image and attitude: Your success in the interview depends on your ability to sell yourself.
5. Responding to and answering questions: When answering questions make sure you pause to show you are thinking about it carefully and give the exact answer. You need to see the difference between questions that demand short answers and long answers. It is very important to be honest about your experience and qualifications. Finally, remember to maintain eye contact and communicate effectively. At the end of the interview, it is good if you have some questions to ask. It shows interest.
6. Time management: Make sure you are not late for the interview. Take extra time just in case.

13.60 What contributes to an effective workplace?

Employees work better when they have a proper workplace that is well designed and equipped. Employers need to bear in mind several aspects, such as the working environment, working relationships, incentives and staff training, in order to provide an adequate work place.

- Working environment: In the travel and tourism industry often the workplace and where visitors interact are the same place (hotel, plane, attraction). The work place needs computer equipment, communications equipment, vehicles for transporting customers and technical equipment. Besides this, the place needs to meet all health and safety regulations. The Working Time Regulations make sure employees do not overwork; they cannot work more than 48 hours a week. Employees working full time are entitled to 5.6 holiday weeks per year, a day off each week, and a 20-minute break per day if they work more than 6 hours. Staff aged 16 and 17 need a 30-minute break and cannot work more than 40 hours a week. Besides the material facilities, motivation is very important for a good job performance. Employees need to feel encouraged to achieve their full potential. Financial incentives and rewards are a good way to motivate employees, who then in turn feel that their contributions are appreciated. Social activities outside work are another way of motivating staff as they can engage with colleagues and feel part of a community.
- Incentives: Incentives can take the form of remuneration, performance-related pay, incentive schemes, pension schemes, perks, and opportunities for promotion and progression.
  1. Remuneration: The National Minimum Wage (NMW) varies according to age. Adults aged 25 or over have a NMW of £7.50; adults aged 21-24 receive a NMW of £7.05; for the ages 18-20 it is £5.60, under 18 years old it is £4.05, and for apprentice it is £3.50. (Data from April 2017).
  2. Performance-related pay: Staff receive pay increases if they perform well. If an employee exceeds their targets over a period of time, they may receive a pay increase.
  3. Incentive schemes: Commissions, bonuses and discounts on products are ways to incentivise staff. Commissions are paid on top of your salary although some sales jobs are commission based only. Bonuses are distributed at a particular time of the year,

at Christmas for example, to acknowledge the employees' annual performance. A successful sale deal can also be rewarded with a bonus.
4. Pension schemes: Pensions are pots of money that can be accessed when one retires. It is very important that employers offer pension schemes to the employees as they contribute towards their future.
5. Perks: Perks can include company cars or discounted travel, free meals, uniforms and use of facilities in a hotel. Employees can also have discounts on tourist attractions, hotels and flight tickets in off-peak seasons.
6. Opportunities for promotion and progression: Knowing that you can be promoted in a company is an incentive if you wish to develop your career.
- Working relationships: Happy employees are far more productive than these who are not. Developing working relationships is key to building a happy work environment.
  1. Management style: There are different kinds of managers with different attitudes towards their employees and management styles. Aggressive employers will demand a lot from their employees and be little appreciative and rewarding. They will also make decisions without considering their employees' opinions. A motivational manager, however, is someone who appreciates the employees' situations and opinions, and works to improve their satisfaction at work. They will listen to their employees' issues, build teamwork and remunerate staff when necessary.
  2. Teamwork: Effective teamwork is important as it is more productive, increases sales and makes people happier. A team leader should know the strengths and weaknesses of the staff he needs to assemble in a team in order to make the team as effective as possible.
  3. Lines of responsibility and channels of communication: It is important to have clear lines of responsibility, authority and communication for the organisation to work well. Decisions need to be communicated, and there should not be any confusion about who gives an instruction to whom. Employees need to know to whom they are responsible and for what. Organisations need to be clearly defined and structured in order to define the lines of communication between one part of the organisation and another, the sources of responsibility, authority, decision-making and accountability within the organisation. They also need to clarify job activities, relationships and responsibilities, coordinate the organisation's activities to help achieve its objectives, and identify the pattern of control for the benefit of internal and external parties.
  4. Equal opportunities: If the staff know that the company is committed to equal opportunities it helps to create harmonious working relationships as no one feels discriminated against. The most typical forms of discrimination job seekers in the tourism industry can encounter are discrimination related to equal pay between men and women, sex discrimination, discrimination of the grounds of disability and race discrimination.
  5. Grievance and disciplinary procedures: Employees are given indications on how to behave at work and what duties to perform. When an employee does not perform properly at work or does not comply with the schedule, his or her supervisor should deal with the issue before the employer steps in. In case of major issues, or if minor issues persist, the manager will need to deal with it and approach the employee. Major issues would include being drunk whilst on duty, committing fraud or assault

or causing damage. In all other cases, dismissal should be the last solution. Usually, however, employees should work with the minimum supervision.

- Training:
    1. Investors in People: Investors In People (IIP) is the national quality standard in the UK for the investment in the training of people to meet companies' goals. IIP provides a framework for improving businesses. It provides a plan to set up objectives and communicate them effectively. People are then trained to achieve these objectives.
    2. Appraisals: Staff appraisal is also called staff development review, and it gives the employee the chance to discuss his performance with his supervisors as well as agreeing a future working plan. A training plan can also be agreed in the appraisal. For the appraisal to be effective it is necessary the careful preparation by both parties, a clear procedure. The appraisal interview should be structured but flexible enough to incorporate new ideas during the review, state objectives and feedback on the work done so far.

Questions

What is meant by sustainable tourism? Why is it very important for most countries of the world?

What data would you need to judge the importance of the tourism sector to the United Kingdom economy?

What are the key organisations in the travel and tourism sector in the United Kingdom?

How has computer technology affected the relationship between the customers and the tourism industry?

Chapter 2

What is meant by serviced accommodation? Why is it important?

What type of market would you expect luxury cruise ships to cater for and what is their importance?

Why might some people like to swap houses for their holidays? What would be the advantages and disadvantages of this?

Why might some people like to visit Center Parks or their equivalent?

Why are demographic factors important when considering demand for tourism?

Why does the demand for accommodation vary according to the season and also vary according to the time of the week?

Why might some universities and other forms of higher education welcome visitors during the holidays? Are there any disadvantages for the colleges?

What are the advantages and disadvantages for tourists of using college accommodation?

What are the likely trends in the United Kingdom for parents and relatives visiting students and vice versa? Why might it be slightly different for Scottish students studying in Scotland?

Why do some families go camping rather than seeking other types of accommodation? What is meant by glamping?

Chapter 3

What are the different types of tour operators?

Why do some tour operators charter aeroplanes?

Why do some people like to visit multiple destinations? What if any are the problems for tour operators trying to cater for this type of demand?

What types of insurance would you expect tour operators to offer?

Why might some customers like rail packages such as those offered by Eurostar? Why might British exit from the European Union alter the demand?

Why might some potential customers like air package holidays?

Why do some customers like to book online for all their tourist arrangements whilst others prefer to go into a more traditional travel agents in the high Street or elsewhere?

Chapter 4
How can tourist organisations best respond to customer needs?

What are the main principles of customer service in the tourist industry?

What are the main communication skills required in the tourist industry?

What are the main business skills required in the tourist industry?

What selling skills are required in the tourist industry?

Chapter 5
Why have increasing numbers of tourists visited the United Kingdom?

What sources of information would you look at when considering the current demand for overseas tourists visiting the United Kingdom?

Why do some UK residents prefer to have holidays in the United Kingdom rather than going abroad?

Why would some tourists (both from the United Kingdom and overseas) welcome the opportunity to have rail-based holidays in the United Kingdom?

Why would some tourists (both from the United Kingdom and overseas) welcome the opportunity to have coach- based holidays in the United Kingdom?

What UK destinations would you recommend to any prospective tourists and why?

Why might some tourists particularly from Australia, New Zealand and the United States of America like some of the English Heritage sites?

Chapter 6
What European destinations would you expect many clients to want to go to in the summer?

What European destinations would you expect many clients to want to go to in the winter?

What are the main European ski resorts?

What Greek and Italian cities would you expect people interested in history to want to go to?

What European museums would you expect tourists to want to go to?

Which European destinations would you expect people who want to experience an interesting nightlife go to?

Chapter 7
Where would people expect to go surfing in the Christmas and New Year period?

What type of tourists would you expect to want to go to Disneyland in Florida?

Why might people need to consult the foreign, and Commonwealth office website?

What is meant by a pandemic? How can people try to avoid these?

What is meant by a Visa?

Why might tourists want to know about exchange rates?

Chapter 8

What are the main functions of marketing in tourism?

Why is it important to consider budget, location and features of the resort?

What are the comparative advantages of direct mail, advertisements in local and national newspapers, local radio and television?

What are the 4P's and why are they important in tourism?

What is meant by branding and how important is it in tourism?

Why is it important to know what your competitors are doing?

What are the comparative advantages of direct marketing and sales designs?

Chapter 9

What is meant by primary and secondary research?

What are the merits of observation when considering tourism?

Why is it important to design good questionnaires?

Chapter 10

In September 2017 there were massive cyclones across the USA. Why were they important and what steps can tourist operators take to try to ensure that their clients are safe?

Why is it important to recognise different time zones?

If an Australian resort is 11 hours ahead of the Greenwich meridian time and it is Friday noon in the UK what time, what will it be showing on Australian clocks?

How can tourist operators try to ensure that their clients do not contract malaria?

Chapter 11

What is meant by green tourism and why is it important?

Why might many countries want to develop tourism especially where there is a decline in the traditional primary industries such as fishing, forestry and mining?

What negative effects can result from tourism?

What is meant by loss of cultural identity?

What role do the public sector tourist organisations play in the United Kingdom?

Why might it be a conflict between property developers and tourism operators?

What is meant by environmental education?

Chapter 12

What are the employment opportunities in traditional high Street travel agent?

What are the employment opportunities in airlines and airports?

Why might it be comparatively easy for some areas to become accommodation providers?

What are the different working patterns in travel and tourism?

What academic qualifications might people consider taking if they want to progress in the tourism industry?

Chapter 13

What skills do employers focus on tourism industry?

What skills do people focus on in the transport industry?

What is meant by DBS's and why is it important?

What is meant by a job description?

What is meant by person specification?

How would you try to test whether someone was a suitable applicant for tourism job?

Why is it important to have clear lines of responsibility in the tourism industry?

What is meant by the term investors in people?

What is meant by staff appraisal?

Index

27869666R00059

Printed in Great Britain
by Amazon